# More Norfolk Churches

## FROM THE AIR

Copyright © 2017 Mike Page and Pauline Young

First published 2017 by Poppyland Publishing, Cromer NR27 9AN
www.poppyland.co.uk

Printed in Europe by Latitude Press Ltd

ISBN 978 1 909796 39 3

A catalogue record for this book is available from the British Library.

Designed and typeset in 10 pt on 12 pt Humnst 777

**Picture credits**

All photographs © 2017 Mike Page

# More Norfolk Churches

## FROM THE AIR

Aerial photography by Mike Page
Text by Pauline Young

Poppyland
Publishing

This book is dedicated to the memory of
Gillian Page
1943-2015
and
John Young
1934-2015

# Introduction

Aerial photographs show churches and every other subject in a different light. One wonders how Pevsner's, the acknowledged authority on church architecture, comments would have changed if an aircraft and photographer had been readily available. He didn't often give opinions and opinions are something which this text writer finds hard to resist especially when the Victorian 'tidy-uppers' are involved as they have been in the majority of our churches. One wonders at the enormous confidence and energy those men had – usually men – and also from where their financial backing came. Change is a costly business.

Moreover Mike Page's pictures represent a collection made over many years together with special requests from the text writer usually as a result of having quite unexpectedly driven past a new (to her) church. In the brief description on each page only those comments which seem relevant to that particular church are mentioned. This isn't a Guide Book – the shops are full of them – this is a different look at our wonderful churches – each one special.

The title of the book indicates that this is a further selection from Mike Page's collection made over the decades. The first *Norfolk Churches from the Air* was published in 2014. We mentioned in that book there are 217 churches in Norfolk listed in the Domesday Book of 1086, and a lot more which are not. Of those still standing some 750 were in existence by the middle of 13th century. Thus this new book is needed to take in another selection!

Norfolk's flint is to the fore in building material. Some stone would be shipped in in medieval times from distant places, even Caen in Normandy, providing perhaps a full face to a tower or just the corners where flint would not do the job. Flint is exceptionally hard wearing, can be used whole as pebbles or 'knapped', revealing an inside surface with varieties of colour ranging from black, through grey or brown to white, all within one stone. Flint has been used in the majority of our churches with the exception of the grander ones.

We made the point that each church is unique. Unique in style, unique in the history that is revealed when one enters the door . There we find brasses from a bygone age, flags from past warfare, rolls of honour carrying names from 20th century conflicts - and sadly now names from more recent military actions.

Since Mike Page began to indulge his passion for flying and photography – at a young age – his pictures have revealed the wonders of the views from above. The high wings of his Mike's Cessna aircraft are especially suitable for aerial photography. We have become more used to such views in recent years, from low orbit satellites, helicopters and much more recently, drones. Each has its own special place; Mike's picture library has a special place because it spans such a long period of time, often tracking the building of roads, of ports, of estates, of architectural gems and practical industrial sites. The collection now contains thousands of images and can be viewed on-line at www.mike-page. co.uk.

The aim of this book is to share or awaken interest in these wonderful buildings which are part of our landscape.

All profits from the sale of this book will be donated to Cancer Charities.

Mike Page          Pauline Young
Strumpshaw         Wymondham

# The Churches

## ALDERFORD St John the Baptist

A common c14 device in this county was to add a buttress to the west side of a thin tower to make it look more substantial, as here. The nave and chancel on the south side are continuous but with a variety of window styles and the most easterly one is blocked up. Inside the church there's a seven sacrament font. These fonts (almost always c15) have been described as 'one of the great treasures of Norfolk churches' and contain on their eight panels the seven sacraments of baptism, holy communion, confirmation, confession, ordination (to Holy Orders) marriage and extreme unction (the anointing of the dying). The 8th panel would contain a similarly appropriate subject such as the baptism of Christ. The reredos (the screen or picture behind the altar) contains images which may have come from the rood screen and although there is no clear division between the nave and chancel the stairs for the rood loft are set in the south wall.

TG 612364 318774
Hall Road, Alderford NR9 5NF

# ANMER St Mary

The church stands close to Anmer Hall, on the Sandringham Estate. There are two fonts, one is octagonal and plain, the other stands in the chapel of the south transept and is of the 'bird bath' type. Neither was used at the christening of Princess Charlotte, the ceremony was held in Sandringham church. The chancel was built c13, the nave followed a century later and the tower a century later still. The grotesques on the chancel gable ends have teeth bared and tongues sticking out, most disrespectful.

TF 573784 329494
The Square, Anmer. PE31 6RW

# ANTINGHAM St Mary

Nicely tucked away along a track stand the two churches dedicated to Saints Mary and Margaret whose ivy covered tower is mostly what remains of a Norman church. St Mary's was begun in the 14th century but when repairs were needed around 1700 then stones were taken from St Margaret's to patch up St Mary's. The reason for there being two churches so close together was because the parish contained two separate manors. St Mary's nave and chancel are continuous but the presence of rood loft stairs indicate that this wasn't always so. The three section south east window in the chancel is a pure pre-Raphaelite trilogy with Mary Magdalene painted by William Morris, the Virgin Mary in the middle by Edward Burne-Jones and Martha (kitchen tools in hand) by Dante Gabriel Rosetti. The River Ant, a tributary of the Bure, rises in the village at Antingham ponds.

TG 625241 332840
Church Lane, Antingham NR28 0NL

## ASHBY ST MARY St Mary

Through the porch there's a magnificent Norman door much like Heckingham's, a short distance away. The rectangle on the outside wall is a c17 memorial too weather beaten to decipher. Inside there's a font similar to Thurton's, a replacement for the original, with a stubby Victorian font cover. The east window contains a small roundel of foreign glass and there's a painted glass reproduction of Holman Hunt's sentimental painting 'The Light of the World'.

TG 632917 302228
Church Road, Ashby Saint Mary NR14 7BJ

## ATTLEBRIDGE St Andrew

The first noticeable feature is that the c14 tower has no buttresses – an architectural device used to strengthen, presumably not needed as the tower is slim with the castle-like crenulations large and spare. Much c19 restoration has left it rather empty inside, there are few wall memorials and the sunlight streams in because there's no coloured glass. The chancel arch is of an unusual almost botanical shape. The font is an elegant substantial piece of stonework and the c17 balusters round the priest's desk wouldn't look out of place in an old country house.

TG 612935 316857
Station Road, Attlebridge NR9 5ST

## AYLMERTON St John The Baptist

Standing in a commanding position on high ground perhaps the theory that round towered churches were built for defence is in this instance not as unlikely as it might seem. A church stood on the site in pre Conquest times but the existing flint building dates from the late 11th century. The upper section of the round tower was rebuilt in 1912 after a doorway was discovered at the tower's base. The porch's upper storey was added c. 1420. Walking round the churchyard one finds the remains of walls and rubble, all that's left of a north transept.

TG 618184 340065
Church Road, Aylmerton NR11 8PZ

# BANHAM St Mary

Spires are uncommon in Norfolk especially in the south of the county. This one is a hundred and twenty five feet high and clad in ribbed lead. The tower and spire were built either simultaneously with the church (c14) or very soon after. The sound holes, traditionally about one third of the way up towers (and whose purpose is to let in light and enable the ringers to hear what they are ringing – not to be confused with belfry openings which are higher up and let out the sounds of the bells ) are in an attractive trefoil shape within a stone circle. Inside, the coloured glass is very fine and the most striking window was designed by the Victorian pre-Raphaelite Henry Holliday – its vibrant colours show Christ in an idealised English landscape with lambs, fruit and sheaves of wheat – lovely but not seasonally accurate!

TM 606338 288208
Church Hill Banham NR16 2HN

## BARNINGHAM NORTHWOOD –
## NORTH BARNINGHAM St Peter

Described as 'a church without a village' St Peter's is now in the care of the Churches Conservation Trust. It contains a tomb chest (John Palgrave d 1611) and an elaborate wall memorial with canopy to Margaret Pope who died on Christmas Day 1624. It also has a monument and brass to the Palgrave family 1516 -1639. One unresolved mystery is a design set in the nave floor, a circle reminiscent of a rose window.

TG 615047 337147
Barningham Road, North Barningham NR11 7LB

## **BASTWICK** St Peter

The church with its c14 tower was used until around the time of the Reformation. Even Pevsner knows nothing more. The tower stands in the garden of a private house where also the bowl of the font was found. It's strange that the tower was left standing – usually it's the first bit to collapse.

TG 643647 318121
Tower Road, Bastwick NR29 5JW

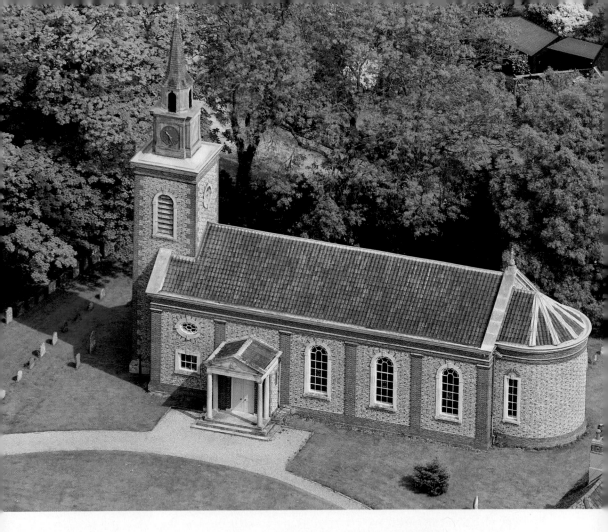

## BAWDESWELL All Saints

In 1944 a Mosquito aircraft returning from Germany crashed on Bawdeswell church killing the two crew members who were struggling to get back to their base at Bexwell (Downham Market). The church was rebuilt in 1950 in neo-Georgian style by J Fletcher Watson. A cross from the old church stands outside the entrance. The church wouldn't look out of place in colonial Virginia, USA.

A connection with Geoffrey Chaucer (The Canterbury Tales) is slightly tenuous. Chaucer was a Norfolkman but why his Reeve is deemed to have come from Bawdeswell has never been explained satisfactorily.

The church's interior was 'facelifted' in 1803 which to some extent renders it bland apart from the fine collection of Preston family (of Beeston Hall) monuments.The tower  and the north wall contain a great deal of carstone especially at the lower levels. The original tower probably predates the Norman Conquest. The nave  and porch were rebuilt for the first time in the c14, the chancel is more lavish in style  and probably followed later..

TG 04661 20907
The Street, Bawdeswell NR20 4UX

# **BESSINGHAM** St Mary

Best described as a 'lovely little church', its character has not been extensively altered by Victorian zeal. The Saxon carstone round tower (one of the earliest in the county) is fairly roughly constructed but it has survived over the centuries. The font has fared less well  and contains several cracks.

TG 16703 37047
Bessingham Road, Norwich NR11 7JP

# BESTHORPE All Saints

Described as having 'a handsome uniformity' the c14 church was seemingly 'not disturbed by the c19 restorations'. The tower is unusual in that it has blocked north and south windows on the ground floor. The north and south transepts are unusually large; in fact the entire church is on a rather grand scale for a fairly small village.

TM 06716 95678
Bunwell Road, Attleborough NR17 2LH

# BILLINGFORD St Peter

There are confusingly two Billingfords in Norfolk (just as there are two Beestons & three Burghs). The other Billingford is St Leonard's near Diss. Unusually here the entire tower is octagonal. Inside there are several special features. The pulpit is stone as is the font which is like no other in Norfolk & has arcading round the bowl. The lectern is 'latten' (an early form of brass), this one is unpolished with a dull finish but has a magnificent and fairly fierce looking eagle perched on a globe. The red brick porch looks slightly out of place with the flintwork of the rest of the c14 fabric & possibly came a little later but the fact that it is there at all perhaps indicates the significance which church porches came to have in the life of churches.

TG 01336 20484
Bintree Road, Billingford, Dereham NR20 4AJ

## BILLOCKBY All Saints

The parish register of the day runs 'Memorandum: that on Thursday ye 15th day of July 1762 there happened a most violent storm of thunder, lightning, hail and long continued rain, by ye violence part of ye roof of ye parish church of Billockby fell into ye said church and broke down ye seats and greatly damaged ye pulpit and desk'.

    Part of the c14 tower had fallen into the nave. Today only the thatched chancel remains having been restored in 1892 when the chancel arch was bricked up. The porch stands alone.

TG 43088 13551
Church Lane, Billockby NR29 3BQ

# BLOFIELD St Andrew and St Peter

The Perpendicular tower is impressive with its fine flushwork on the buttresses, three light belfry windows and an enormous window above the west doorway. The easternmost bay on the south side of the nave has 'slipped' hence the huge buttress outside and a large transverse arch in the aisle inside. The porch connects with the south aisle and housed the village school for years. On the north wall inside is a monument (1630) to Edward Paston, his wife and nine children and above it a Tudor helmet. Does the helmet add gravitas or was it that no other home could be found for it? On the magnificent font, maybe c14, are depicted scenes from the Life of Christ – unusual subject matter for a font. But most impressive of all are the modern (1936) stained glass windows, a memorial to Margaret Gordon Harker of Blofield Hall who was Director of the Norfolk Branch of the British Red Cross. The pictures mainly have nursing themes but a favourite is that of the Scottish fisher girls gutting herring at Great Yarmouth.

TG 33526 09241
Church Road, Blofield NR13 4NA

# **BRACON ASH** St Nicholas

The 'lump' on the north side of the chancel is the Berney Mausoleum, the entrance to which (inside the church) contains sculpture similar to the magnificent Bedingfield monuments in Oxburgh church. There's no tower. It is speculated that there never was one and when the bell cote fell down it was replaced by the present bell supported on a frame next to the south door. The church has a large number of hatchments (diamond shaped boards displaying coats of arms), unusual for such a small church.

TG 17950 00200
School Road Bracon Ash, Norwich NR14 8HJ

# **BRADWELL** St Nicholas

St Nicholas church has changed from being a remote country church to becoming a place of worship in a bungaloid suburb of Great Yarmouth. And it changed counties from Suffolk to Norfolk in a 1974 boundary reorganisation. There's been a fair bit of Victorian 'improvement' inside. Outside, ancient and modern are close together with the Norman round tower only a few yards away from the recent addition of function rooms. Of particular interest inside the church are on the font the lion with metal still embedded (the work of iconoclasts?), the 1930's stained glass memorial window to brother and sister shipbuilders and the richly carved communion rail which clearly began life in a country house and contains sea monsters and 'barley sugar' balusters.

TG 50302 03837
Church Walk, Bradwell, Gt Yarmouth NR31 8QQ

## **BRANCASTER** St Mary

Pevsner considers the chancel to be the earliest part of the church, the c15 substantial tower came a century later. The four large clerestory windows make this a church full of daylight. The stone font is somewhat plain but this is offset by a particularly intricate and high font cover. The font stands at the west end of the church with a backdrop of what remains of the resited roodscreen, behind which is the tower door. By far the most interesting item inside the church is the 'preacher's dial' – a clock mounted high on the west wall where it could be seen only by the preacher when delivering his sermon and not by the congregation unless, conspicuously, they turned their heads! There's only one other in Norfolk and that's in St Mary's, Long Stratton. Simon Knott notes that the churchyard contains headstones of victims of a c18 shipwreck (much like Happisburgh further round the coast).

TF 77238 43886
Saw Mill Road, Brancaster. PE31 8AJ

## BRANDISTON St Nicholas

The chancel has been pulled down and the Norman round tower is not in line with the nave suggesting that it might have been attached to an earlier church on this site. Its octagonal top was built in 1890 because the original had fallen. The church is now in the care of the Churches Conservation Trust.

TG 14130 21413
Brandiston, Norwich NR10 4PJ

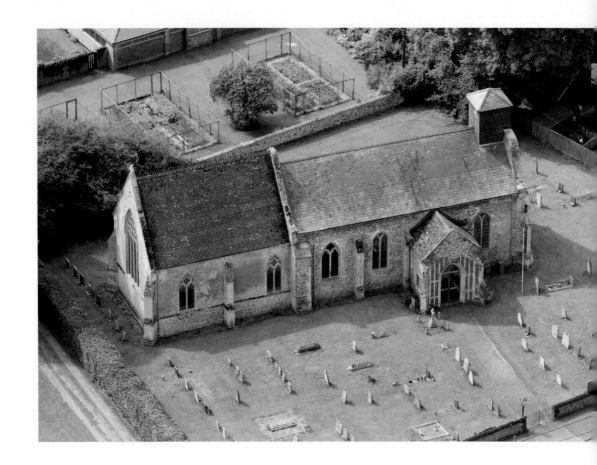

# BRIDGHAM St Mary

This church has an odd profile. The chancel roof is higher than the nave and the bellcote is boarded up, the single bell now housed near the rood stair. The outline in the west wall indicates that there was once a tower. The porch originally consisted entirely of flushwork but there's been a great deal of patching up in red brick. The door from the porch sags with age and the step is hollow from use. The font has a Jacobean cover and depicts the Assumption – quite rare – the only other one in Norfolk is at Great Witchingham.

Grid RTL 95759 85850
The Street, Bridgham, Norwich NR16 2RY

## BROOKE St Peter

This round tower tapers towards the top which has an unusual twelve sided chequer design parapet. Inside is one of the rare Seven Sacrament Fonts (there are only twenty two in Norfolk). Brooke's has a 'step up' for the priest. A great many architectural styles become apparent in a walk round the outside of the church – the nave has Perpendicular windows, the chancel's belong to the Decorated period except for the Tudor (flattened top) windows. The Porch's magnificent outer door looks Early English and the red brick buttresses are almost certainly Victorian. Of particular interest inside the church are angels supporting the font (as at Salle), an hour glass stand near the pulpit (with glass intact) and a poor box fixed to the last pew. Three or even five locks on a poor box are not unusual – and each lock always had a different keyholder – but actually to anchor the box to the pew seems to be security taken to the extreme.

TM 29391 99540
The Street, Brooke NR15 1JX

# BUNWELL St Michael and All Angels

Here's another magnificent flushwork porch, a tribute to the flint knappers' skill. This is an entirely Perpendicular (c15) church but sadly the nave and chancel have had to be cement rendered on the outside. Inside the church there's a hanging rood of Christ on the cross with Mary mother of Jesus and St John on either side. This is a WW1 war memorial but sits (or rather hangs) a little strangely as traditionally the rood would have stood in a rood loft framework with access from stairs at ground level. The original intention of the pre-Reformation rood loft was to separate the nave and chancel. Although rare there's a surviving rood loft at Attleborough.

TM 12550 92750
Old Turnpike, Bunwell, Norwich NR16 1TF

## BURGH-NEXT-AYLSHAM St Mary the Virgin

The church is in a wonderful setting with the River Bure only a few yards off picture to the south. There's a seven sacrament font but it's not in good condition. Unusually, as the roof line shows, there's a step down into the chancel.

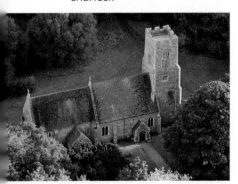

TG 21774 25082
Church Lane, Burgh, Norwich NR11 6TR

# BURLINGHAM St Peter

This ruined church is situated in a cottage garden near to the present church of St Andrew, North Burlingham. The collapse of the round tower in 1906 eventually brought about the church's closure due in part, no doubt, to the proximity of St Andrew's. Some of the fittings were removed to St Andrew's and the benches went to Blofield according to Adrian Pye who requests also that permission is sought of the garden's owner before viewing.

TG 36837 10053
Main Road, North Burlingham, Norwich NR13 4TA

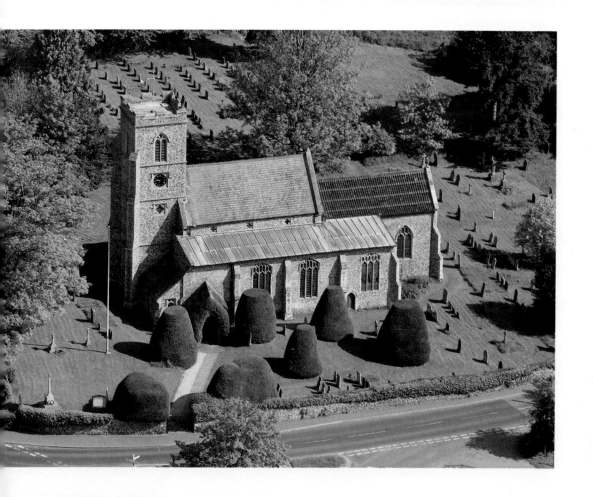

## **BUXTON** St Andrew

There doesn't seem to be any religious symbolism attached to the neatly cut yews in the churchyard but certainly they appear to be rather more manageable than when left to assume their natural shape and height. The Victorians have used their customary energy to 'improve' the church but they have chosen to leave a touching memorial to Mary Ann Kent who died in 1773 age four under inoculation (sic) . Her parents' anger manifests itself in the remaining part of her memorial; *her fond parents deluded by prevalent Custom suffered the rough officious hand of Art to wound the flourishing root of Nature and rob the little innocent of the gift of life.* The 'prevalent custom' wording is intruiging because although innoculation had been practised by the Chinese for centuries Edward Jenner didn't introduce the small pox vaccine into England in 1798, more than twenty years after the child's death.

TG 23348 22694
Mill Road, Buxton NR10 5JE

# **BYLAUGH** St Mary

From the outside the church looks rather bleak but inside all is harmony and free from 'Victorian interference'. Some box pews are at the crossing and the three decker pulpit is considered to be the best in the county.

TG 03609 18381
Bylaugh, Dereham NR20 4QE

# **CAISTOR** St Edmund

When the church was built (c13/14) the Roman town (Venta Icenorum) had ceased to be, leaving only a pile of bricks. The bricks were used in subsequent centuries to patch up the church. Inside it is mainly modern(ish) with a lovely 1930's pulpit except for faint traces of wall paintings including that of St Christopher which, unusually, is on the south wall – generally he's on the north wall so that entering through the south porch the traveller is greeted by him. The conclusion is that in this church the north door provided the entrance. In fact looking at the picture there appears to be no obvious porch. In the churchyard stands the Victorian grave of Georgiana Docking out of which grows a huge oak tree. Simon Knott in his funny and slightly irreverent way (www.norfolkchurches) wonders if she was buried with an acorn in her pocket!

TG 23234 03385
Stoke Road, Caistor St Edmund, Norwich NR14 8QL

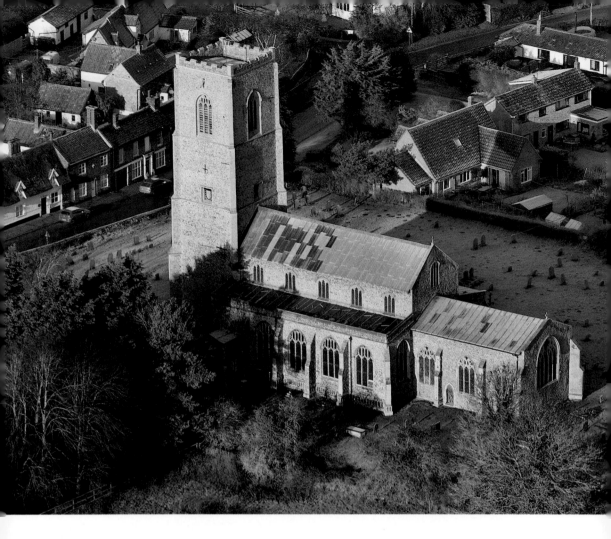

## **CARBROOKE** St Peter and St Paul

This a stately church with a grand ninety-nine foot c15 tower with a flint flushwork base which extends all the way round to the chancel. It has a clerestory on both the north and south sides. Both porches are of special interest too, the north has a parvise (an upper floor) and the south an ogee arch (concave changing to convex) framing the door. Close by is the site of a c12 Knights Templar religious house, the only one of its kind in the country.

TF 94977 02225
Church Street, Carbrooke, Thetford. IP25 6SW

## CARLETON ST PETER St Peter

There's no road to the church just a grass track. There is a notice in the porch with words to the effect of 'Don't bother to think about stealing the roof lead here because it's been stolen already'. Very sad. But the belfry stair of the c16 tower remains and is in full view in this picture. And the churchyard is cared for.

TG 34056 02273
Ferry Road, Carleton St Peter, Norwich NR14 7BD

# **COLKIRK** St Mary

The c14 tower is unusually placed being on the south side of the church. There's a Norman font on chubby legs but nothing else pre Reformation and the Victorians have been busy with their usual reforming zeal.

TF 91775 26546
Church Road, Colkirk, Fakenham NR21 7NZ

## COLTISHALL St John the Evangelist

This view looking onto the north aspect of the nave and chancel is unable to show the two Saxon windows under the eaves sitting above the 1865 circular window. The c15 tower is the newer structure, the nave and chancel being Norman or Saxon. Entrance into the church is through the tower, the north door is blocked.

TG 27150 19777
Church Street, Coltishall, Norwich NR12 7HE

# **COLTON** St Andrew

The church is delightful and largely of the 13th and 14th centuries (except for where the Victorians re-roofed the church, added buttresses to the chancel and restored the porch.) Inside on the west wall there's a faint c14 wall painting depicting two women gossiping - a deadly sin in an innocent age.

TG 10443 09339
Church Lane, Colton, Norwich NR9 5DE

## CRANWORTH St Mary

The adjacent villages of Cranworth and Southburgh both have spires in a part of the county where spires are uncommon. Which came first? The answer is, as usual, complicated. Southburgh dates from the 13th century but the Victorians did an almost complete rebuild. Cranworth dates from the 14th century and is almost intact with very few Victorian 'improvements'. The church is full of memorials, mainly to the Gurdon family one of whom fought at the Battle of Naseby on the Parliamentarian side.

TF 98287 04468
Church Lane, Cranworth, Thetford. IP25 7SQ

## CRINGLEFORD St Peter

It's hard to believe from its appearance that this church has Saxon origins. The clues are that in the nave and chancel there are windows which have the splay both inside and out and when the rood stairs were demolished in 1898 some Saxon stonework was discovered. This is a well attended church on the edge of Norwich but do the congregation know that parts of the church in which they're worshipping were here before the Domesday Book was compiled and that other features appeared before the Battle of Hastings was fought?

TG 19833 05834
Newmarket Road, Cringleford, Norwich NR4 6XL

## DENVER St Mary

Standing nicely in the middle of the village this carstone church was begun in the 13th century, four hundred years before Vermuyden began draining the Fens  and built the first sluice across the river here at Denver. The church is in a slightly elevated position, those early church builders knew a thing or two about flooding. The c13 tower had a spire until a gale in 1895 blew it down. Inside the church the nave roof has been boarded at some time but the original wood bosses depicting flowers have remained – a nice touch.

TF 61442 01638
Ryston Road, Denver. PE38 0DP

# DICKLEBURGH All Saints

This church would be imposing in a town setting but it seems especially so in a village. It's large, the tower has battlements, the nave has a clerestory and the porch is an outstanding example of decorative flintwork. The tower is unbuttressed.

TM 16784 82419
The Street, Dickleburgh, Diss IP21 4NQ

# DUNSTON St Remigius

Hethersett, Roydon and Seething churches are also dedicated to St Remigius who is traditionally portrayed with a dove - an unlikely story about a dove who got him out of a difficult situation, as in the stained glass panel here at Dunston.

TG 22847 02243
Stoke Lane, Dunston, Norwich NR14 8PE

# EARSHAM All Saints

The nave is probably Norman (with later additions) but the tower dates from the 14th century as does the chancel. One of the treasures of this church is the seven sacrament font, the panels are defaced but still recognisable as mass, penance, matrimony, extreme unction, the crucifixion, baptism and ordination. The c19 reredos behind the altar is considered to anticipate the work of Ninian Comper (Wymondham Abbey). Of the monuments there's one to the Hon Colonel Windham who distinguished himself at the Battle of Blenheim (1730).

TM 32598 88810
Church Road, Earsham, Bungay NR35 2TQ

## EAST BILNEY St Mary

The church is at least half a mile from the village, why? Did the plague come to an earlier village (as fire had come to Cley) necessitating a move away? This 14th century church was practically wholly rebuilt in the 19th century. Neglect over a period of time and damage to the tower during Kett's Rebellion (1549) had taken its toll. Clearly it wasn't a happy church – in the south window there's a memorial to Thomas Bilney who was burned at the stake for his religious beliefs in 1531.

TF 95621 19562
Fludges Lane, Beetley NR20 4HW

# EAST RAYNHAM St Mary

Although it appears older this church was built in 1868. The £7,000 cost was borne by the Marquess Townshend  and the Reverend Charles Phayre. It's a copy of the original c14 church which contained an Easter Sepulchre. There are thirty-three Easter Sepulchres in Norfolk (the best being at Baconsthorpe, Kelling  and Northwold). Easter Sepulchres stood on the north wall of the chancel  and received an effigy of Christ at Easter  and held the host (the communion bread) between Maundy Thursday  and Good Friday. Easter Sepulchres largely disappeared at the Reformation. Of the original church in addition to the Sepulchre, the c15 font, a parish chest of 1602 and in the floor a brass commemorating George Townshend who died as a boy in 1500 remain. There's an 1852 relief monument to Lord Charles Vere Ferrars Townshend. And a ring of eight bells.

TF 87961 25542
East Raynham, Fakenham NR21 7ER

# EAST RUDHAM St Mary

Church towers have a habit of collapsing as did East Rudham's in 1876 bringing down most of the rest of the church. So what we see today is a rebuild reusing the fallen material. In a glass case at the western end are displayed the plaster fragments of a reredos  and there are other salvaged remainss such as the unidentified c13 coffin lid which was found in the graveyard. But generally the rebuilt church is rather bare.

TF 82730 28270
Bagthorpe Road, East Rudham, King's Lynn PE31 8RA,

# EAST WINCH All Saints

A prominent buttress on the tower contains a staircase giving access to the parapet, note the buttress' pinnacle which is more substantial than the remaining three. The sanctus bell, which used to be rung during Holy Communion at the point where the bread and wine were offered up by the priest, also has a distinctive pinnacle. The church is mainly in the Perpendicular order of architecture (1350-1550) although in the north aisle there are two 13th century coffin lids. There have been many alterations to the interior including an 1875 remodelling by Sir Gilbert Scott (Norwich RC Cathedral) and a font cover (1913) by Ninian Comper (Wymondham Abbey and Great Ryburgh). The c15 font itself bears the coat of arms of the Howard family, Dukes of Norfolk.

TF 69132 16265
Church Lane, East Winch, King's Lynn PE32 1NQ,

## ELLINGHAM St Mary

A few more yards and this church would be in Suffolk on the other side of the River Waveney. The river was an important means of transport until fifty or so years ago. During the last century wherries plied up to Walker's Maltings in Bungay and inside the church there's an illuminated Roll of Honour listing the sixty or so Walker's employees who were casualties of WWI. The church was begun in the 13th century but the ugly c18 red brick staircase fastened onto the outside of the tower and providing a staircase to the belfry looks somewhat odd and uncomfortable. Inside the church there's a quantity of c19 and c20 stained glass, a nicely carved stone tribute to the two churchwardens of 1853 and an extraordinary stone carving of a bishop with an elongated neck, possibly the c12 one who consecrated the church.

TM 36622 91855
Mill Pool L:ane, Ellingham, Bungay NR35 2EP

## FILBY All Saints

The tower is spectacular. It has elaborate flushwork on the stepped battlements with the four Latin Doctors – Ambrose, Augustine, Jerome and Gregory – theological rather than medical, in statue at the corners. Inside the church the rood screen vies in splendour with that of Ranworth.,

TG 46915 13220
Church Lane, Filby, Gt Yarmouth NR29 3HW

# FINCHAM St Martin

Almost totally rebuilt in the 15th century this grand church stands in the middle of the village. The south side (facing the street) is the more imposing and below the clerestory are pinnacles, battlements and flushwork and there are battlements to the chancel. The north face is plainer, the clerestory windows are of two lights only and no battlements. Inside there are angels; the roof is made of alternating tie beams and hammer beams where lodge the angels. There are grotesques in the carving too – all thought to be the work of one man and executed around 1488. Much of the work is thought to have been paid for by the wealthy Fincham family. Various furnishings including the fine square font came from another church in the parish, St Michael's, which disintegrated when the tower fell during a marriage service in 1745.

TF 68798 06427
High Street, Fincham. Kings Lynn, PE33 9EJ

# **FISHLEY** St Mary

This little church stands on a mound in a clearing surrounded by fields. The Victorians tidied it up somewhat although earlier 'improvers' added height to the tower using Tudor bricks.

TG 39805 11501
Fishley, near Acle NR13 6DA

# FLEGGBURGH aka **BURGH ST MARGARET**
## St Margaret

Virtually the entire church has been rebuilt – a giveaway being the spick and span and 'standing to attention' appearance except for the cottage style dormer window above the porch – definitely an unusual feature. What a pity that the church's Norman origins are apparent only in the north and south doorways.

TG 44516 13976
Main Road, Fleggburgh, Gt Yarmouth NR29 3BF

## FORNCETT ST PETER St Peter

The Saxon tower is very fine  and has an unusually large number of openings with a doorway into the church at the base. The Victorians have been busy inside the church but their finely crafted bench ends rival the c15 ones, some of which remain. In the north aisle there's a c15 alabaster table tomb, the wife wearing a kennel headdress in the fashion of the period.

TM 16480 92833
Aslacton Road, Forncett, Norwich NR16 1LT

# FOULSHAM The Holy Innocents

An unusual dedication. The church along with the rest of the village centre suffered a devastating fire in 1770 so every feature except the stonework is more recent. The one hundred (almost) foot tower is particularly impressive (Pevsner calls it 'ambitious') with its battlements and crocketted pinnacles. Impressive also (and equally ambitious?) is the large number of clerestory windows. The c20 font cover is huge and spectacular and rather than having to raise such a large structure for a christening it has opening doors at its base.

TG 03228 25057
Hindolveston Road, Foulsham, Dereham NR20 5RX

# FOXLEY St Thomas

This church's greatest treasure is its rood screen which, on close inspection, shows a turbulent period in English church history. Before the falling out of Henry VIII with the Church of Rome, rood screens were the norm. They separated the clergy in the chancel from the congregation in the nave. The rood (Christ on the cross, his mother Mary and St John on either side) stood on a beam (the loft) below which a painted screen and doors provided a barrier. Stairs gave access to the loft. At the Reformation everything changed. Henry's son Edward VI ordered the removal (the sawing off) of the rood and rood loft. Under his successor, the Roman Catholic Queen Mary, the top was reinstated only to be removed again under Elizabeth I. Here at Foxley the rood screen bears the marks of its attachment to the rood and rood loft. The screen has retained much of its beauty and when closed the doors reveal paintings of the four Latin Doctors (see also the tower at Filby).

TG 03933 21704
The Street, Foxley, Dereham NR20 4QP

## FRITTON (near Morningthorpe)
## St Catherine

In this church it's possible to see what a rood loft actually looks like. Although the lower panels are the originals the new loft was built in 1900 and connects to the stairs which makes it all so much easier to understand. There are faded wall paintings but the happiest (!) factor in the whole church is the font where the lions and angels are all smiling.

TM 22927 93253
The Street, Fritton, Norwich NR15 2QU

# GATELY St Helen

This 15th century church is idyllically situated. Sitting well back from a country road with only a grass path leading to it there's a house in front thereby offering a degree of security. The tower is substantially buttressed. The eight 15th century rood screen panels depict lesser known saints including Sir John Schorne holding a little boot with a devil peeping out and a saint rejoicing in the name of Puella Rideborne. Insects, e.g. a caterpillar adorn the pew ends. An inscription slab to Mrs Elizabeth Segrave declares 'she was a Person of good standing and Just Principal (sic) but in Conjugal Life not so happy as Deserving'- whatever that implies.

TF 96036 24466
Church Road, Gateley, Dereham NR20 5EH

# GLANDFORD St Martin

In 1896-99 Sir Alfred Jodrell of Bayfield Hall recreated on the original site a copy of the former c15 St Martin's church which had been in ruins since the early c18. The craftmanship is superb, the woodwork especially so. The whole has the feel of Anglo-Catholicsm which reflected the faith of his mother Adela Jodrell, in whose memory the church was rebuilt. Curiously Sir Alfred chose Letheringsett as his final resting place.

TG 04377 41474
Glandford, Holt NR25 7JR

## **GREAT CRESSINGHAM** St Michael

The church stands on a mound surrounded by modern houses. The exterior is flint in entirety which gives it a uniformity lacking in some churches. The frieze above the south door contains the letter M displayed in decorative form with crowns above, the M presumably standing for the St Michael to whom the church is dedicated. The land on which this church stands was owned by Norwich Cathedral and the Erpingham Gate into the Cathedral Close was designed by the designer of the frieze here, James Woderofe

TF 85171 01769
Priory Drove, Great Cressingham. IP25 6NJ

# GREAT HOCKHAM The Holy Trinity

This is a large church up a track next to the parkland of Great Hockham Hall and well away from the present village which suggests the devastation of the Black Death (bubonic plague c14 which decimated communities all over Europe). Apart from the tower which fell (as towers tend to) c17 and has been replaced with a bell turret, most of the rest was built c13-c15. Wall paintings abound and there are some lovely medieval bench ends (a mermaid as at Upper Sheringham, a contortionist, two bears and a couple of gnomes). Unfortunately the door is locked much of the time, presumably because of the church's remote situation.

TL 95068 92091
Hockham Hall, Great Hockham. IP24 1NZ

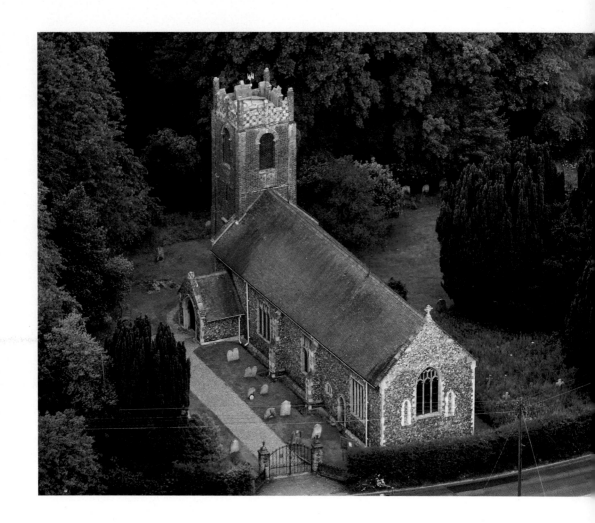

## GREAT PLUMSTEAD St Mary

There's very little of the original c15 church left. The new tower with its distinctive chequered top was built in 1711 and the rest was restored in c19. Its older neighbour at Little Plumstead is equally heavily restored. Clearly those eager Victorians had the Plumsteads on their 'to do' list.

TG 30210 09957
Church Road, Great Plumstead, Norwich NR13 5AB

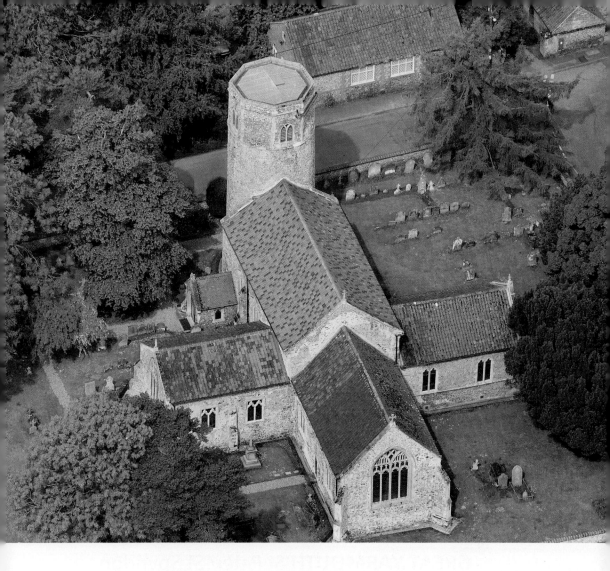

## **GREAT RYBURGH** St Andrew

This church has so many noteworthy features that it's hard to know where to begin. A cruciform church with a round tower is in itself a rarity. The Saxon tower (i.e. built before 1066) has lumps of conglomerate at its base. The tower's octagonal belfry stage was added in the 14th century. A latter addition also was the south porch (1891). The font with a Victorian cover is framed by a round Norman arch. The Victorians made rather a lot of changes including lowering the floor. But most noteworthy here are the works of Gothic Revivalist Sir Ninian Comper whose work includes some stained glass in Westminster Abbey and the reredos (altar screen) of Wymondham Abbey. In St Andrew's he made changes to the chancel ceiling, brightly coloured in his day but now dramatically painted white. A visit is an uplifting experience.

TF 96181 27271
Mill Road, Great Ryburgh, Fakenham NR21 0DZ

# GREAT YARMOUTH St Peter/ St Spyridon

It's not often that churches change their dedicated saints, although North Walsham did at the Reformation, but a decline in the Anglican congregation and an influx of Greek Cypriot workers resulted in this transition. St Peter's was built of yellow brick and flint by local church architect J.J. Scoles in 1831 at a cost of around £8,000. The houses surrounding it came later. Pevsner described the building as 'large and uncommonly dull'. A new lease of life was injected in 1964 by the Greek Cypriot community who dedicated the church to St Spyridon. The tower originally had pinnacles which were removed as early as 1860 on the grounds that they were dangerous. Victorian Health and Safety.

TG 52703 07106
St Peters Road, Great Yarmouth NR30 3AU

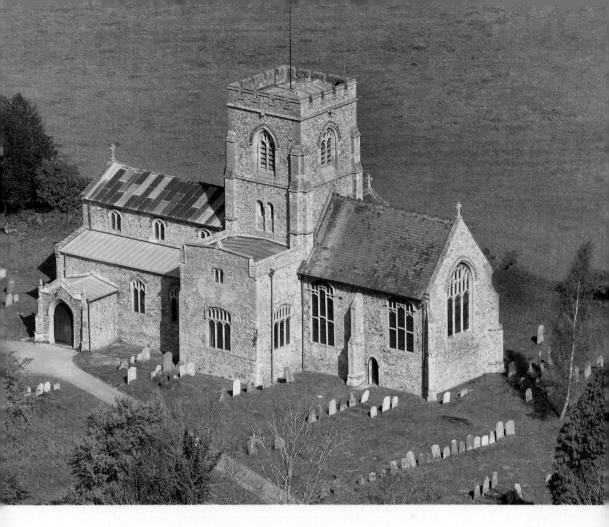

## GRESSENHALL St Mary

This rather majestic church of Norman origin with its cruciform plan stands alone outside the village. The clue to its age is the typical Norman double window-opening in the tower. The top third of the tower with a single window on each face was added in c15. The Hastings double height chapel is at the south transept. Inside the church the rood screen panels have been moved and are badly defaced but on a positive note there's a ledger stone in the chancel with the charming inscription:

'Here resteth the Body of Robert Halcot
of Gressenhall, Yemon, hooe departed
this life the 2 day of November Anno
Dom 1640 Him have wee for a time lost
who bilt this gallery att his oune cost.'

TF 95953 15478
Barn Lane, Gressenhall NR19 2QQ

# GRISTON St Peter and St Paul

There's elaborate detailing in the flushwork of the tower which was rebuilt in 1477. The sanctus bell at the east end of the nave was rung to tell workers in the field that it was time to stop and pray. There's an embellishment at the top of the tower with the crossed keys of St Peter and the sword of St Paul. Possibly the most distinctive feature of this church is the indentation of the top rail of the c.17 communion rails, identical to that at nearby Thompson so probably made by the same carpenter. And a look at the first poppy head on the north side will show a face with eyes looking both ways – creepy.

TL 94260 99307
Church Road, Griston, Watton. IP25 6PY

# GUESTWICK St Peter

This configuration is most unusual, there's not another one like it in Norfolk but there's an explanation. The tower, most of it, was part of an earlier church of cruciform shape and dating from the 11th century. When the church was rebuilt (c15) the nave and chancel were added mainly southwards and the tower was heightened. And the Victorians did their little bit of tidying up in the shape of a new nave roof.

TG 06143 27017
Church Lane, Guestwick, Dereham NR20 5QH

# GUIST St Andrew

The church, probably begun in the 13th century, had become somewhat neglected over the centuries and we have the Victorians to thank (yes, really!) for its preservation.

This was mainly under the supervision of the Diocesan Architect. Some original parts remain such as the Tudor windows in the nave and the c14-c15 tower, note the harmonious way the belfry staircase blends with the rest of the tower as opposed to the red brick eyesore at Ellingham. The carving round the pulpit rim is notable especially for the green man, a pagan symbol of fertility who appears in various places in some Norfolk churches.There are three locks to the Jacobean parish chest with 1636 carved on the front. Three locks were mandatory, one for the priest and one each for the two churchwardens so that all three had to be present when it was opened.

TG 00031 25559
Norwich Road, Guist, Dereham NR20 5NS

# HACKFORD St Mary

St Mary's is the parish church of Hackford near Wymondham rather than All Saints, Hackford in Reepham of which only a stone wall remains. The unusually small 'windows' in the tower are the sound holes. Most towers have them and their purpose is not to let the sound out as might be assumed but to enable the ringers to hear what they're ringing and also to let in light, although the holes here are so small it's doubtful that they could do much of either. Around the porch there's some fine flint flushwork and in the porch itself next to the sturdy entrance door there's a c15 holy water stoup with a high stone canopy – it looks much like a font. Simon Knott (www. norfolkchurches.co.uk) wonders if it could have arrived here from nearby Wymondham Abbey. Most striking inside the church are six stone steps which would have led to the rood loft.

TG 05914 02233
Church Lane, Hackford, Wymondham NR18 9HN

# **HALVERGATE** St Peter and St Paul

Thanks to a thorough restoration of 1874 there's not a great deal of historic interest within the church except a stained glass picture of St Christopher and a palimpsest brass in the chancel. Palimpsest brasses were those where both faces had been inscribed in turn i.e. recycled. Brasses were discontinued when monuments became fashionable. On the tower are two sets of small sound holes separated by a height of about 15 feet. It seems to have been a very common practice to extend the tower upwards sometimes hundreds of years after it was built, as the change in the stonework here demonstrates. At the base of the tower there's some attractive flint flushwork.

TG 41755 06668
The Street, Halvergate NR13 3PL

## HARDINGHAM St George

It's the opinion of Mortlock and Roberts in their *Guide to Norfolk Churches* that the appearance of the c13 tower is spoiled by bricked battlements. Be that as it may this is a very elegant church although the tower looks slightly odd being tacked onto the nave part way along. The western end of the nave serves as a War Memorial, particularly to those who died in WWI.

TG 03489 05115
The Old Hall, ChurchRoad, Hardingham, Norwich NR9 4EW

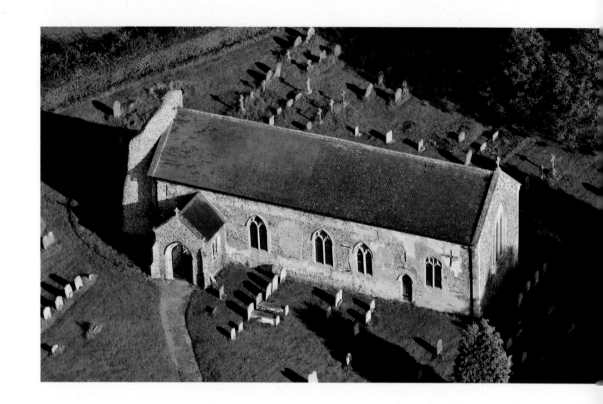

# **HARDWICK** St Margaret

The 'lump' on the western end of the church is what is left of a round tower lost in a storm 1770. Mainly this is a Norman church  and very simple inside and out. The rood screen is in remarkably good shape although the figures have been more or less destroyed. The rood stairs don't actually go anywhere now but it's still possible to visualise them going all the way to the rood. This church is a little gem.

TM 22304 90086
CommonRoad, Hardwick, Norwich NR15 2SP,

# HASSINGHAM St Mary

It's hard to imagine the simplicity which will be found inside this church. The peace and calm has been created by sympathetic restorers following a dramatic fire in 1971. The whole now has the 'feel' and sparseness of a school chapel with modern furnishings all in a light wood. Adrian Pye who has visited every Norfolk parish church (see Bibliography) sees things differently and of the modern altar table he says it 'looks as if it came from IKEA'. Everyone to his own opinion but it's a blessing that the restoration wasn't needed a hundred years earlier when we might have had gloomy imitation of medieval craftsmanship as in so many of our churches.

TG 36887 05540
Church Road, Norwich NR13 4HH

## HEDENHAM St Peter

The Victorians have been here in force. This church is overly ornate, the chancel being described by Mortlock and Roberts (*Guide to Norfolk Churches*) as 'uninhibited Camden Society Gothic'. The Camden Society was named after the antiquary William Camden and not after the London borough. The highly influential Society which was well established by the mid c19 looked back to the high ideals of Gothic architecture especially in an ecclesiastical context. And the cement rendering outside is a shame too.

TM 31198 93345
Church Road, Hedenham, Bungay NR35 2LF

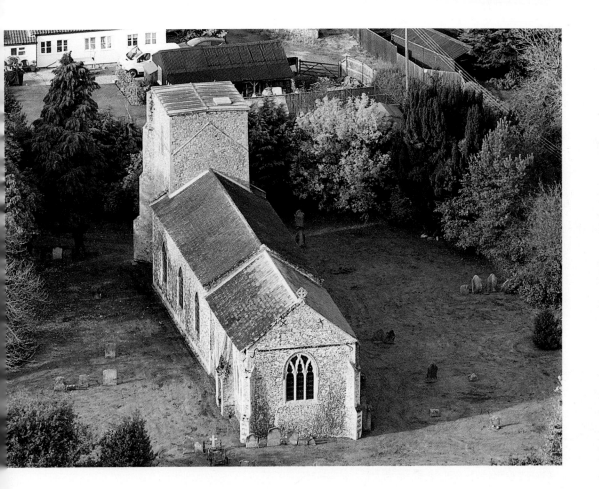

## HELHOUGHTON All Saints

To say this church has been 'messed about' is an understatement. For reasons unknown the tower was decapitated by about a third  and a sound hole was enlarged to become a bell opening. In the 1780s north  and south aisles were demolished together with the clerestory windows. By 1990 a restoration was under way and a light and airy church has been created. The most extraordinary feature is the font. To describe it as 'huge  and chunky' is an understatement. Certainly it doesn't fit in with the restored church – it would be hard to find a church where it did fit in.

TF 86883 26498
The Street, Helhoughton, Fakenham NR21 7AH

# HELLINGTON St John the Baptist

For a church to become redundant then to be taken into the care of the Churches Conservation Trust it has to be something special. Church historians consider that this church is architecturally more significant than many of those close by. The round tower is Norman (the battlements were added later) as is the tall, richly carved south door. The north door is Norman too but much plainer, most of the rest is of the 14th century. Corbels abound, they're inserted into the masonry to be load bearing but, so as not to waste a perfectly good surface, often they were decorated with faces or figures of fun or foliage. The porch is extraordinary, it contains what normally we'd consider to be windows but there's no evidence that they were ever glazed. There had been clerestory windows as can be seen in the picture but these were bricked in at a later date. Inside the church there's evidence that the screen was moved. Why were all these changes made? Tantalisingly we shall never know.

TG 31383 03059
Hellington Hill, Norwich NR14 7BS,

# HEMBLINGTON All Saints

This is just a little country parish church but, in its usual place on the north wall (when it is there at all) is a huge c15 painting of St Christopher not only in traditional pose with a child in his arms, but also containing other scenes from his life. It was discovered in the 1930's and is considered to be among the finest in this country. Unusually the font too has paintings on its panels. The Norman round tower has a curious little cap.

TG 35273 11536
Church Lane, Hemblington, Norwich NR13 4EF

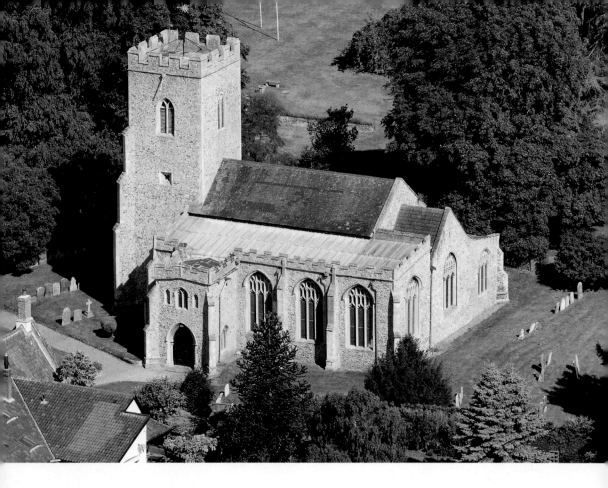

# HEMPNALL St Margaret of Antioch

This is a church like no other. Outside it is solid and almost square, the chancel has all but disappeared following two fires centuries apart. There are Saxon 'remnants' in the north side of the tower but the church was built mainly in c13 and c14. Inside, the modernity is striking. The pulpit has been removed to a corner and presumably sermons are delivered centre stage. A modern spiral staircase uses the space at the base of the tower to lead to a meeting room at first floor level. The whole is light and bright and welcoming. Although the pews have been succeeded by chairs, not every piece of church furniture has been replaced. The font, possibly of c14 origin, was defaced by Parliamentary soldiers who were billeted in the village during the Civil War but enough of it remains to be considered handsome. This is a well cared for church.

TM 24071 94459
The Street, Hempnall, Norwich NR15 2AD

# HEMPSTEAD St Andrew

There are two Hempsteads, one near Holt (All Saints) and one between Stalham and the sea. This is the latter. The church's great treasure is its screen. The painted panels at the base contain images of lesser known saints including St Juliana, St John of Bridlington, St Elgius whose panel was stolen in 1982 and St Theobald – all in a sorry state. St Juliana has the devil on a halter except that he looks more like a cartoon character lying puppy-like on his back waiting to have his tummy rubbed. The top half of the screen is a wonderful tribute to the woodcarver's art.

TG 10509 37027
Church Lane, Hempstead, NR12 0SH

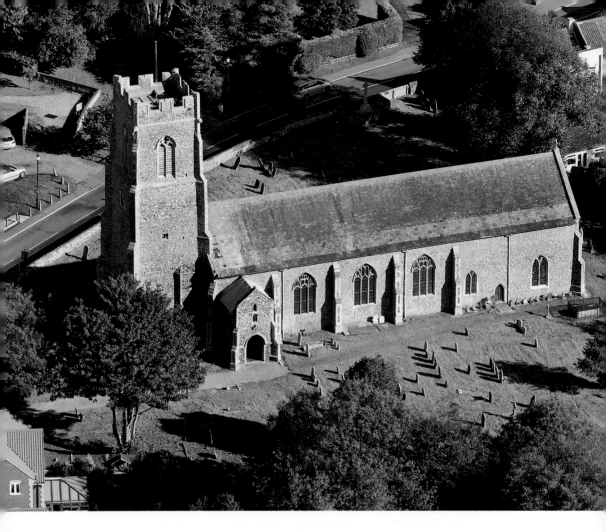

# HEMSBY St Mary

A print of 1840 shows the church with a fine Jacobean screen, a three decker pulpit and box pews … but that was before the Victorians got to work on it. Now it's heavily restored. The chancel has a window of 1908 showing St George and a woman knitting.

TG 49378 17379
The Street, Hemsby, Great Yarmouth NR29 4EU

# HETHERSETT St Remigius

There are four Norfolk churches dedicated to this unusually named saint, the others are at Dunston, Seething and Roydon. This is an impressively grand church with a large congregation. The c14 chancel had been in ruins since the

Reformation but was rebuilt in 1898. The nave roof when reconstructed was done in two parts with different levels (best appreciated from an aerial picture!) The tower with its nicely proportioned small spire has buttresses tapering in seven stages giving it a neat and graceful appearance.

TG 16005 04938
Norwich Road, Hethersett, Norwich NR9 3AJ

# HEYDON St Peter and St Paul

Heydon is a pretty and 'self contained' village (there's only one way in and out) and all centred on the village green. There was a church here in c13 of which the font survives. The font is plain, rounded and wouldn't look out of place as a garden ornament. Most of the church was built c14 but the tower came a century later. In 1970 repairs revealed a wall painting whose subject was part of the medieval 'The Three Living and Three Dead' sequence which gives the message 'As I am now so shall you be'.

TG 11353 27403
The Street, Heydon, Norwich NR11 6RQ

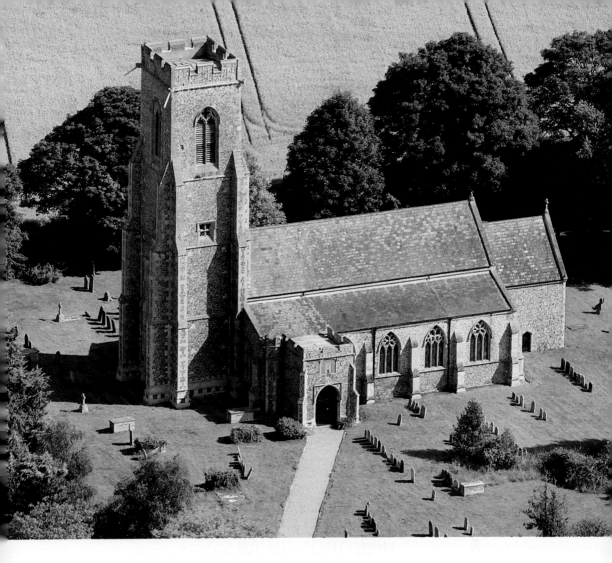

## HICKLING St Mary

The church was begun a couple of centuries after the Black Canons founded the Augustinian Hickling Priory on the edge of the village. But whereas the Priory was victim of the Dissolution (1536) and was abandoned to become a ruin where some remains stand in a farm yard, the church is well maintained. It's been the victim of a bit of graffiti during the Civil Wars and some c19 restoration.

TG 41471 24201
Town Street, Hickling, Norwich NR12 0BQ,

## HILBOROUGH All Saints

Once found (along a track not signposted) this church is magnificent. The tower is especially grand with wonderful flushwork and elegant proportions with pierced stone and crocketting to add a final flourish. The windows of the clerestory and nave rather outshine the chancel. There's a fine west door with intriguing figures carved in the spandrels (the triangular space between the curved arch and the supporting brace). One is of a bearded man holding aloft a severed head, the other is a smartly dressed young man but he's missing an arm. The south porch is a chequerboard of stone and flint. The east window has attracted criticism for having strips of gaudy glass around it. But this church also has an extraordinary connection between the Duke of Wellington and the Nelson family of whom seven were some time rectors, including Horatio's father Edmund who left Hilborough to become rector of Burnham Thorpe where Horatio was born. The Duke of Wellington lived for a while at Hilborough Hall, home of his son, and worshipped in the church.

TL 82538 99954
A1065, Hilborough, Thetford IP26 5BU,

## HINDRINGHAM St Martin

This is a grand but heavily restored church. The tower was the first part to be restored – rebuilt rather – because it fell down shortly after it was built in 1386. The most spectacular item is a wooden chest claimed by experts to have been built 1175-1200 (late Norman) – the earliest known parish chest in England. It's believed to have come from Binham Priory at the Dissolution.

TF 98414 36383
The Street, Hindringham, Fakenham NR21 0QB

# HONING St Peter and St Paul

The most extraordinary feature of this church is the chancel which was reduced in size in 1795 and more resembles an alcove rather than the most spiritual part of the church – even Pevsner is puzzled. The buttress at the eastern end of the nave is more substantial than the other four as are the two which support the chancel. From the inside the abbreviated chancel doesn't look as odd as it does from the outside.

TG 32685 28000
Long Lane, Honing, North Walsham NR28 9QW

## HORNING St Benedict

The church is dedicated to St Benedict as is St Benet's Abbey, a short distance downriver. But whilst the Benedictine abbey was founded before the Norman Conquest the church began life three centuries later. The exterior north wall bears evidence of arcading which once supported a north aisle. On the c14 tower battlements stands a figure at each corner rather than the usual pinnacles. A visit here is worthwhile especially to see the grotesque carving on the bench ends, particularly the one of the devil pushing a man down into hell.

TG 35480 16615
Church Road, Horning, Norwich NR12 8PZ

# HOUGHTON in the BRAKE St Martin

Sir Robert Walpole moved the village away from the (possibly part c13) church to New Houghton so that he could build Houghton Hall  and create a deer park. He added the tower in 1730, the top third of which is considerably smaller than the rest. There are also c19 additions. The remains of both Robert Walpole, England's first Prime Minister  and his youngest son Horace (man of letters are laid to rest in the vault. The latter was influential in popularising the Gothic form of architecture by enlarging a small cottage at Twickenham into a building of grand proportions at Strawberry Hill)

TF 79229 28408
Houghton Hall, Houghton, King's Lynn PE31 6UE,

# HOUGHTON IN THE DALE St Giles

There are several Houghtons in Norfolk, Houghton on the Hill near Swaffham and Houghton in the Brake (in Old English a *braec* is a thicket) aka New Houghton on the edge of Houghton Hall. This Houghton is in the dale near Fakenham. Houghton in the Old English translation here means 'a settlement (*tun*) on a spur of a hill' or on a hill slope. The rood screen contains the (mutilated) faces of some lesser known saints (St Emeria, St Mary Salome and Saint Silvester). It's greatly to their credit that when churches suffered restorations during the last half of c19 the restorers left the rood screens untouched so we can judge for ourselves the destructive zeal of Edward VI and (subsequently) Cromwell's vandals. The church was for the most part rebuilt in the 1870s but by using the original materials it avoids looking too new.

TF 92364 35344
The Old Parsonage, Houghton St Giles, Walsingham NR22 6AQ,

# HOVETON St John

A Norman church stood here evidenced by carstone quoins at one corner at the base of the nave. The red brick tower (1765) replaced an earlier one which fell, as towers have a habit of doing. There's much Victorian restoration – I wonder why they painted the c15 rood screen brown? (heads should roll). There's some lovely medieval glass including a window showing St John with the devil peeping from his chalice.

TG 30961 18186
Horning Road, Hoveton, Norwich NR12 8NY

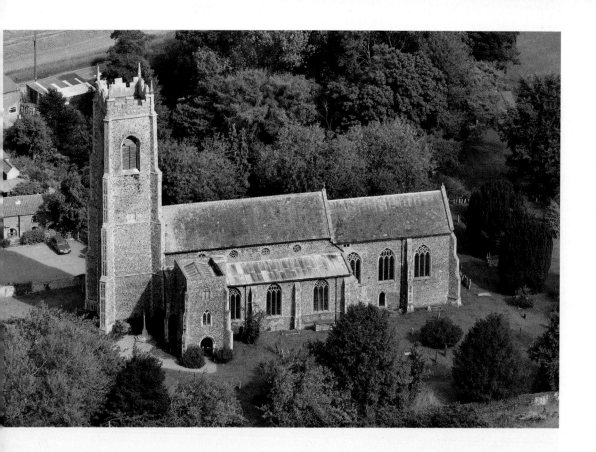

# INGHAM Holy Trinity

This is a rather splendid church with an impressive four stage tower, elaborate buttresses, pinnacles and a very interesting history. In 1355 the Pope gave Sir Miles Stapleton permission to rebuild the derelict church, derelict following the Black Death, and establish a priory of Trinitarian canons next to the church. The order, the only Trinitarian order in Norfolk, lasted until the Reformation (1536). Fragments of the priory remain next to the church. The porch is rare in having three storeys – the parish priest, who was also the Priory Sacrist, lived on the upper two floors. The clerestory windows are of an unusual design with elaborate tracery. Simon Knott (see Bibliography) likens it to a kaleidioscopic effect. The screen too is unusual being made of stone, its purpose here was to keep the monks separate from the rest of the congregation.

TG 39070 26020
Mill Road, Ingham, Norwich NR12 9AB

# INGOLDISTHORPE St Michael

In the churchyard there's the stump of a preaching cross where the resident priest or a wandering friar would preach to an outdoor assembly, easy to slip away if the content was uninteresting!. The church dates from c14 but the stone font is earlier. Originally the font was square but clearly it has been 'octagonalised' – I wonder why? The rood screen, whilst now sadly without its base of painted saints, contains intricate carving above.

TF 69056 32753
Manor Close, Ingoldisthorpe, King's Lynn PE31 6PB

## INGWORTH St Lawrence

This is just about the prettiest looking church there is. The abbreviated round tower together with flint and thatch stands on a small mound by the road side. The Norman tower fell in 1822 and now with a conical thatch cap serves as the vestry. The nave was rebuilt late c14 when the porch was added. High on the porch stands a mass dial telling a medieval congregation when it was time for Mass – there are several churches with Mass dials in Norfolk. The octagonal font looks a bit battered and the rood has been painted with what looks like dark varnish but there's a crucifix in place. The Royal Arms of William and Mary are splendidly executed and a great contrast to the faded and dusty hatchments of other monarchs in some churches. And there are box pews.

TG 19264 29626
Cromer Road, Norwich NR11 6PD

# **INTWOOD** All Saints

It is difficult now to believe that in the 16th century this c13 church with a mainly Saxon tower was a neglected ruin  and used as a sheep shelter. But Henry Hobart (creator of Blickling Hall) restored it  and added the octagonal top to the tower using material from the equally derelict Keswick church nearby. More restoration was carried out by the Victorians including interestingly carved bench ends, particularly in the chancel.

TG 19700 04174
Intwood Road, Intwood, Norwich NR4 6TG

# IRSTEAD St Michael

This is a lovely mainly c14 church with Norman origins and one could conjecture that the thatch for the roof always has been carried in by reedlighter on the River Ant nearby – possibly even from the reedbeds of the How Hill Estate a couple of miles downriver. The corner stones for the tower came by river from the quarries at Barnack in Northamptonshire. The church would not have been considered grand enough to bring stone over from Caen in Normandy as happened for Norwich Cathedral. Inside, the rood screen contains paintings of apostles and there's evidence of a small stair which would have led to a rood loft. The handrail to the pulpit contains a carving of a small head and fig leaf which is believed to have come from nearby St Benet's Abbey, presumably at the Dissolution. On the north wall, as was the custom to greet travellers coming through the south door via the porch, there's a faint drawing of St Christopher.

TG 36546 20462
Shoals, Irstead, Norwich NR12 8XS

# **KENNINGHALL** St Mary

Described as a c15 town Kenninghall, now regarded as a village, was a place of some importance. One time seat of the Dukes of Norfolk, the third Duke promised a spire for the church tower but when he was detained in the Tower until the death of Henry VIII on charges of treason the spire never materialised. Kenninghall Palace (now demolished) was the some-time residence of Henry VIII's daughters Elizabeth and Mary in turn during the reign of their half brother the young Edward VI. Curiously the nave has a set of clerestory windows but no aisle to justify their construction. The high font cover must have been splendid although it has seen better days.

TM 04110 85968
Church Street, Kenninghall, Norwich NR16 2EN

## KIRBY CANE All Saints

A round tower and a decorated rounded stone doorway are giveaway signs of a Norman or an even earlier church together. There's an interesting c14 stone font and stairs to a former rood loft – ingredients for a lovely little country church, which this is. There have been some later additions – the pulpit is c17 as are the elegant communion rails. Unusually there are two modern hatchments (one belonging to Lord Berners, the other to c20 churchwarden Raymond John Crisp – presumably of Crisp Maltings). Next door is the Hall where Oliver Cromwell rested on his way to Great Yarmouth to sort out a little local difficulty. The night stop must have been interesting for all concerned because the owners of the Hall were staunch Royalists.

TM 37396 94146
Loddon Road, Kirby Cane, Bungay NR35 2HN

# LAMAS/LAMMAS St Andrew

The tower belongs to c15 but most of the rest is a c19 rebuild using the original materials on the extant foundations. Surprising then that the church 'weeps' i.e. the chancel is out of line with the nave, a surprising six feet to the north in order to reach firmer ground.

TG 24532 23217
The Street, Lammas with Little Hautbois, Norwich NR10 5JQ

## LANGLEY St Michael

The nave seems particularly long in relation to the chancel. A Saxon church stood on this site prior to its c14 building and renovation c19. Sadly the three decker pulpit has gone as have the box pews, replaced by more ordinary looking benches. Whilst in no aspect is this church spectacular it has a comprehensive collection of medieval glass brought over from Europe by the local landowners, the Beauchamp-Proctors. The Dowager Lady Beauchamp-Proctor saw which way the wind was blowing during the French Revolution and arranged for some of the c16 glass from Rouen Cathedral to be whisked away to Langley for safekeeping. A wise move as it turned out because two of Rouen's magnificent rose windows were destroyed in WWII. Similar glass appears also in Chegrave church. A considerable degree of understanding appears on the WWI memorial board. Those men who lost their lives are listed centre panel but 'those who came back' (harmed no doubt physically or psychologically or both) also are named on the boards either side.

TG 35490 00929
Langley, Norwich NR14 6BL

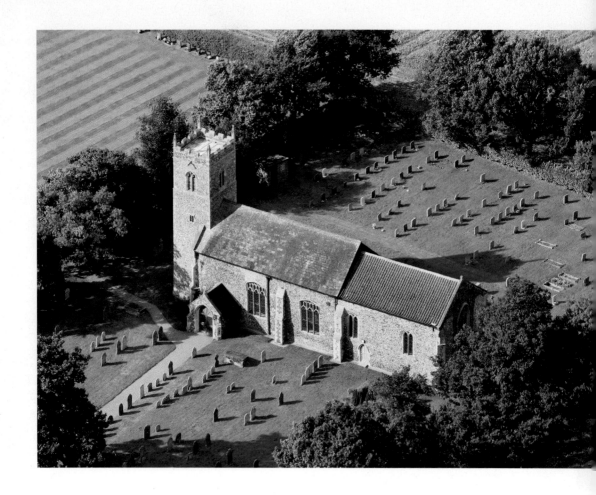

# **LINGWOOD** St Peter

The nave is c13 as is most of the tower. The chancel and top third of the tower followed a century later, so all in all this is a lovely old church in the area of Norfolk which has a high concentration of medieval churches. A faint head and shoulders of St Christopher is on the north wall and the c15 benches have quaint figures on the ends.

TG 36063 09004
Church Road, Lingwood, Norwich NR13 4AP

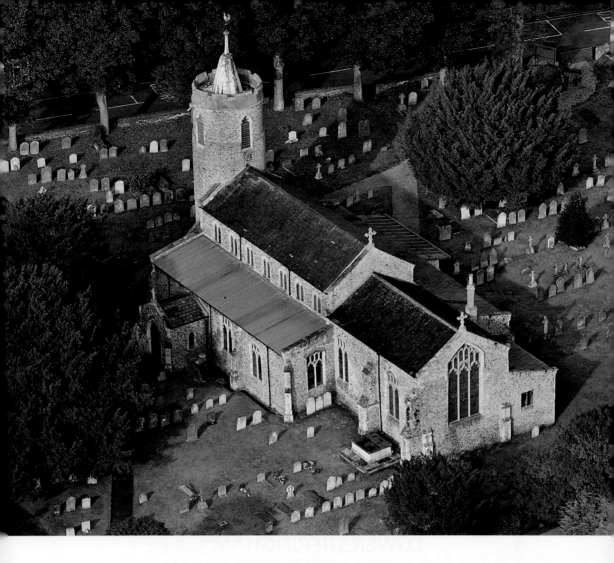

## LONG STRATTON St Mary

The spirelet adds distinction to the Norman round tower but came later. The two arcades were added c14 together with the clerestory windows. The font cover is Jacobean as is the pulpit. On the west wall is a clock, large enough to be read from the pulpit, possibly to tell the parson he'd gone on long enough. There's a similar one in Brancaster church. At the rear of the church stands 'the Sexton's Wheel' . The rules for its operation seem complicated . It's a device for determining the day on which a penitent parishioner should begin a fast. There's no answer to the question 'Why'? It resembles a large bicycle wheel minus tyre, divided into eight quadrants with a leaf  and fleur de lys design in each – except there's no flower in the last quadrant – perhaps it's fallen off. There's only one other Sexton's Wheel in existence – in Yaxley church, Suffolk.

TM 19650 92277
Ipswich Road, Long Stratton, Norwich NR15 2TA

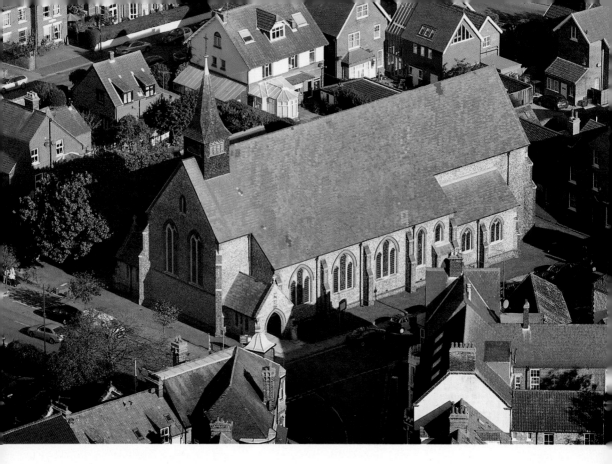

## LOWER SHERINGHAM St Peter

Until the coming of the railway (1887) and the consequent popularity of the seaside, Lower Sheringham was just a fishing village. The main population was concentrated on the higher ground and on the medieval church of Upper Sheringham (*Norfolk Churches from the Air*). The modernising zeal that the Victorians wreaked upon old churches comes in for much criticism (including from the writer) but here, in a new build entirely of their creation, they got it absolutely right. The church is large, light and welcoming. Initially the daughter church of All Saints Upper Sheringham, St Peter's foundation stone was laid on St Peter's day 1895 by Mrs Caroline Upcher on land in the centre of the town donated by the Upcher family . It has a red brick and flint exterior and a slate roof. The wide nave was designed for chairs rather than pews, there's a plain stone font and the pulpit and lectern are carved from oak. The church is a meeting place and concert venue – a welcome return to some of the purposes of the original places of worship.

TG 15696 43217
Church Street, Sheringham NR26 8QS

## MAUTBY St Peter and St Paul

Mautby was the childhood home of Margaret Paston and to where she returned after her husband's death. Her correspondence with her husband (absent at court) written around 1420 has become important historical source material known as 'The Paston Letters'. The contents of her letters to him painted a picture of the domestic life of the time, his to her of the politics of the court. Several of her ancestors have tombs in this church.

TG 48060 12357
Church Lane, Mautby, Great Yarmouth NR29 3JA

## MERTON St Peter

Up the drive towards the Hall then park on the grazing in front of this beautiful church with its round tower which has been there centuries longer than any other building in the area. The tower is probably pre-Conquest. On entering it's immediately apparent what great beauty is in the woodwork especially in the rare three sided altar rail – there are only two others in the whole of Norfolk (at Thurning and West Dereham). The two decker Jacobean pulpit stands very close to the front pews, no possibility of falling asleep during a long sermon here. In the foreground of the picture lies Merton Hall, most of which burned down in 1956; to the left is the gatehouse (built 1620).

TL 91236 98136
Thompson Road, Merton IP25 6QJ

## MIDDLETON St Mary

A goodly proportion of this 15th century church is of carstone, a commonly used building material in the west of the county where it is excavated  and often referred to as 'gingerbread' for visual reasons. Only two panels of the rood screen remain but in the chancel there's evidence of the rood stair. Much more in evidence are mice – the scourge of churches – but this time they're the work of master carpenter Robert Thompson of Kilburn, Yorkshire, who carved a mouse on every object he crafted. He died in 1955 but in his workshop the tradition continues to this day. Here in this church are the only examples of his work in Norfolk. The communion rails, a table, prayer desks  and the lectern all display a mouse 2"-3" long – not always easy to spot.

TF 66283 15986
Station Road, Middleton, King's Lynn PE32 1RA

## MILEHAM St John the Baptist

There's the base of a Preaching Cross in the churchyard. Preaching crosses functioned in the times when the churchyard was a market or gathering place and where the incumbent or itinerant preachers would preach the Word of God. Since the church is within the village it would seem a suitable site for working the crowds. The positioning of the tower is unusual but it was the last part to be built – almost as if someone had forgotten to allow for it. The huge buttresses are made of concealed concrete and there have been subsidence problems, hopefully resolved. The church's greatest treasures are in its c14 and c15 glass  and its modern East Window – a millennium project showing John baptising Jesus Christ in an English countryside. Unusual but the colours are lovely.

TF 92147 19646
The Street, Mileham, King's Lynn PE32 2RD

## MORSTON All Saints

When the tower was struck by lightning in 1743 it was repaired somewhat unsympathetically with red brick, but that has stood for nearly 300 years. The gem inside the church is the 1480 rood screen with the four Latin Doctors (Ambrose, Augustine, Gregory and Jerome) and opposite four evangelists – all lined up and unharmed by the subsequent 'reformers' intent on stamping out idolatry.

TG 00846 43860
The Street, Morston, Holt NR25 7AA

## MOULTON ST MARY St Mary

This beautiful little church is now in the care of the Churches Conservation Trust. The Norman tower is the earliest part  and given the church's lonely position even today, then defence could have been one of the reasons for building the tower. The nave  and chancel date from c13. The south entrance door is medieval with wrought hinge straps across its whole width  and whilst on the subject of doors Mortlock refers to 'a large priest's door in the chancel'. Now maybe priests were large – visions of Friar Tuck – but a priest's large door reads better. The c13 font was of Purbeck marble – the fashion of the day  – and the walls are rich in paintings including those of St Christopher together with 'The Seven Works of Mercy' (food to the hungry, drink to the thirsty, welcome strangers, clothe the naked, visit the sick, visit prisoners) a c13 sequence similar to the one at nearby Wickhampton.

TG 40207 06603
Reedham Road, Norwich NR13 3NW

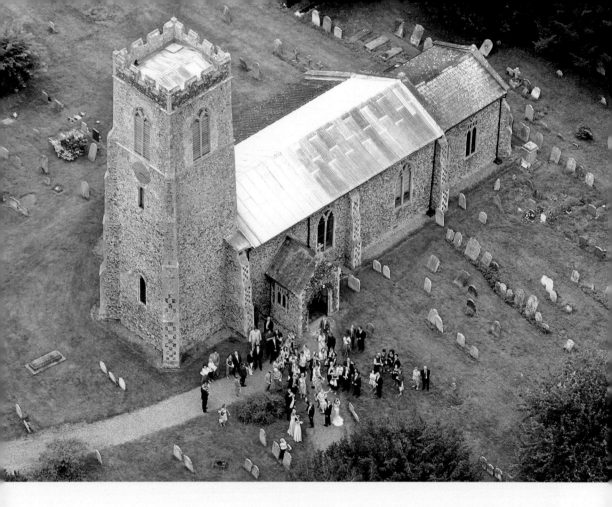

## MULBARTON St Mary Magdalene

How wonderful to have an aerial photograph among your wedding pictures!
The church has an excellent early glass collection but how unChristian it is to
have obtained it if not by deception, then by stealth. A c19 curate at Martham
acquired the living here and brought with him some of the glass with Old
Testament themes. Adam is portrayed digging in the Garden of Eden with a
facial expression more of endurance than of pain (it's likely his back hurt!).

TG 19391 01139
The Common, Mulbarton, Norwich NR14 8JS

# MUNDHAM St Peter

The population of Mundham is small and there's another church, Seething, nearby. And, until 1749 when it was declared redundant, yet another church St Ethelbert's (c13/14) was also in the parish. The very small remains of St Ethelbert's are now hidden in foliage. St Peter's tower has distinctive flushwork on the battlements and prominent gargoyles enable the escape of water. The Norman south doorway carries fine botanical decorations but the rest of the church has been subjected to 'improvement' over the centuries. A modern item is the font and it replaces a broken square Purbeck marble Norman font abandoned nearby.

TM 32469 98010
Loddon Road, Mundham, Norwich NR14 6EJ

# NEW BUCKENHAM St Martin

The church (begun 1246) is dominant in this large and pretty village/small town  and its majesty quality is due perhaps to John Coke who in 1479 left money for leading the roof. The Perpendicular tower has huge crocketted pinnacles on chequerworked battlements. The three-light belfry windows have flattened Tudor arches  and the tower's base course has carved panels and flint flushwork which extends round the porch. There's flushwork too on the buttresses  and the porch is battlemented with griffins on the corners. The clerestory windows match the Perpendicular aisle windows. The outside is a visual feast. The inside has been described as 'nobly proportioned though rather austere'. The nave's hammer-beam roof contains carved heads of the twelve apostles  and the shaft of the font contains elongated lions and woodwoses (wild men). In the chancel there's a rare Easter Sepulchre cum tomb which may be that of the church's founder Sir Robert de Tateshale.

TM 08789 90547
Church Street, New Buckenham, Norwich NR16 2BA

## **NEWTON FLOTMAN** St Mary

Mortlock states that a thoroughgoing restoration in the 1890's renewed almost everything (those well meaning Victorians again). The stepped battlements are the only distinguishing feature of this country church.

TM 21296 98503
Church Road, Newton Flotman, Norwich NR15 1PP

## NORTH WALSHAM St Nicholas

This is a grand town church, large, impressive and until the Reformation was dedicated to the Blessed Virgin Mary. The ruined tower used to be 147 feet high but on May 16 1724 the west and south sides fell bringing down, also, the steeple but 'no-one getting any mischief'. A further storm of 1836 caused another collapse - no reports of anyone 'getting any mischief' that time either. A vestry has been created in the base. There's a tall and impressive 15th century painted font cover – font covers were used to prevent the theft of holy water for witchcraft. Two miserichords are on display, one represents a king and the other a woodwose (a green man or wild man who, as legend proclaims, bathed in the river of eternal life which turned him green). There's so much to see in this church and be sure not to miss Sir William Paston's tomb near the altar. He's wearing richly embossed full armour and has a large shield containing the Paston family coat of arms.

TG 28309 30280
Market Place, North Walsham NR28 9BT

# NORTON SUBCOURSE St Mary

This is an area of marshes criss-crossed by dykes which drain eventually into the River Chet, a tributary of the Yare. It can feel isolated round here but some of the earliest churches are in this now remote part of Norfolk. Norton is common enough, it means the north *tun* or settlement (north of what we don't know). Subcourse is thought to mean 'on the river'. The round Saxon tower (which is not central to the nave so probably was part of an earlier church) is topped with a brick margin. When in 1380 a college of secular priests transferred here from Raveningham the nave and chancel were remodelled and the roof is now in a continuous line The plain marble font is decorated only with blank arcading and the rood screen is no longer there. The church is smaller now than it was in 1795 when the north aisle was demolished. Entering the nave one walks on the old cracked pre Reformation *mensa* slab (altar top – thought perhaps to be deliberately disrespectful

TM 40781 98642
Church Road, Norton Subcourse, Norwich NR14 6RU

## OVERSTRAND St Martin

Church congregations increased here as Overstrand, Cromer and the surrounding area became popular holiday destinations at the turn of the twentieth century. The roof of the original church had collapsed in the c18 leaving just part of the nave and the c15 tower. In 1867 Christchurch was built nearby. In 1911 the original church was restored and enlarged and Christchurch was demolished – a bit like the old bike which over time had new wheels, new tyres, new handlebars but was still the same bike. And the church had a rival in the village. In 1898 the Methodist church had a splendid new chapel designed by Edwin Lutyens who was at the height of his creativity. The previous year he'd adapted The Pleasaunce as a holiday home for Lord and Lady Battersea (with the garden laid out by Gertrude Jeckyll) and in 1899 built Overstrand Hall for banker Lord Hillingdon.

TG 24068 40753
Cromer Road, Overstrand, Cromer NR27 0NT

## OXNEAD St Michael and All Angels

The tower is described as 'good looking' having stepped battlements and a decorative base course. The Lacon mausoleum north of the church and off picture has been described as 'looming like a wartime bunker, surmounted by an uncompromising cross'. The monumental tomb for Admiral Clement Paston is not as grand as that for his relative Sir William Paston at North Walsham.

TG 22981 24056
Oxnead Hall, Oxnead, Norwich NR10 5HP

## PULHAM MARKET St Mary Magdalene

Pevsner's first comment is that the church is 'quite big with a strong west tower'. No arguing with that. Mortlock and Roberts state it's a 'very grand looking church' no arguing with that either. There's elaborate flint flushwork on the north porch. The money for building the porch (twenty shillings) was left in the will of John Intwode 1540's. Inside the church it's almost pure Victoriana ( there was a big restoration in 1873) especially the stained glass windows – the design was a forerunner of the Pre-Raphaelite style. Over the chancel arch there's a wall painitng of the Ascension. There's also some c15 and c16 glass. The whole in its setting has the appearance of a grand town church rather than the quiet village which Pulham Market has become.

TM 19699 86089
Harleston Road, Pulham Market, Diss IP21 4TA

## REPPS St Peter

The parish is also know as Repps with Bastwick or Repps cum Bastwick

The base of the tower is Norman, the ornamental belfry was built c13 and the battlements added two hundred years later. The brick porch belongs to the c17 and the brick chancel c18. And the Victorians had a go at a later date with the chancel windows. Nikolaus Pevsner who generally is so precise with his descriptions and dates merely says of the rood rcreen 'Not much of it is old'.

TG 42189 16915
Church Road, Repps, Great Yarmouth NR29 5JS

# ROCKLAND St Mary

Not to be confused with Rockland (aka Rocklands) All Saints and Rockland St Peter, both near Attleborough. This Rockland is over to the east of the county near Surlingham and not to be confused either with the ruins of Rockland St Margaret with which it once shared a churchyard. The slim c14 tower is tapered and there are Tudor (straight tops) windows on the south side of the nave. The east window shows Mary with the infant Jesus and below it a reredos with panels possibly from the rood screen. This church is light and bright and with the Royal Arms of Queen Victoria hanging there as a Seal of Approval.

TG 31186 03979
Rectory Lane, Rockland St Mary, Norwich NR14 7EY

## **ROUGHTON** St Mary

Lyn Stilgoe (*The Round Tower Churches of Norfolk*) has explained the reason for bands of a slightly different colour in the stone at ten feet intervals. A winter activity, when frosts made building impossible, was to gather up the next year's supply of flints  and if they came from a different place then they might well be a different colour. Ten feet of tower building was a reasonable amount in the frost free months of each year. This tower is almost certainly Saxon because of the characteristics of the lowest level where conglomerate (aka puddingstone – a mix of stone, pebbles  and ironstone) were laid in a herringbone pattern.

TG 22026 36538
Church Loke, Roughton, Norwich NR11 8SZ

## RUSHALL St Mary

Described as 'basically a Norman church which has been rebuilt' (Adrian Pye). The octagonal top was added to the base of the tower at a later date, later perhaps because of the intervention of the Black Death. But by 1733 the church was reported to be in a very bad condition. Entering through the porch to the south door there's a mason's mark at low level on the door jamb, there's a sturdy table (Stuart period) which serves as an altar and an ornate desk (possibly Spanish) given to the church in the 1930's. The one bell in the tower was hung for full circle ringing.

TM 19785 82659
Langmere Road, Rushall, Diss IP21 4UD

## SAHAM TONEY St George

The tower, completed 1497, has enormous three light belfry windows and fairly big sound holes in fact the whole church is on a large scale. Surprising then that the priest's door from the churchyard into the chantry is so small. The extensive work carried out in c15 may well have been a restoration rather than a rebuild because there are also medieval bench ends to the pews including some 'funny lion elbow rests' (Mortlock). There's a modest font but a magnificent Laudian font cover so named after Archbishop William Laud of Canterbury (1633- 45) who wanted Protestant reforms but without austerity (he meant well but lost his life in the process). The elaborate font cover stands high and has a pelican (the sign of piety) at the top.

TF 89956 02017
Pound Hill, Saham Toney, Thetford IP25 7HN

# SAXLINGHAM NETHERGATE St Mary

A church which has a longer than usual entry in a guide book is bound to be full of interest and so it is here. The Perpendicular tower has a sundial and an (intentional) one handed clock. The earliest stained glass found anywhere in Norfolk is in the chancel, made c13 it's in the south chancel window, four medallions depicting Saints John and James, a beheading of a person unknown and the martyrdom of St Edmund. There's slightly later (c14 and c15) glass in the chancel. The church has a large collection of window glass generally, possibly some from elsewhere including from the church at Saxlingham Thorpe half a mile away, abandoned in 1688. A striking WWII memorial triptych window contains not the usual list of names (as does the Honours Board for WWI near the Rood Screen) instead the central figure of St George is flanked by RAF pilot's wings and Winston Churchill's 'Never in the field of human conflict'. It says it all. There's the usual robust c15 font (possibly from the other church?) with the typical happy looking lions round the base and very fine wood carvings on the pulpit and on the top half of the Rood Screen. Left of picture is the Parsonage by Sir John Soane 1784.

TM 23135 97193
The Street, Saxlingham Nethergate, Norwich NR15 1AJ

## SCARNING St Peter and St Paul

In the 1850's Thomas Jeckyll (much in demand as a church restorer) changed the pitch of the c15 roof so that he could economise by tiling with slate rather than the more costly lead – if only other Victorian 'improvers' had followed suit then lead thieves today would be out of business. There's quite a lot of flamboyance in this spacious church. Both the tall font cover and the screen have been (in modern times) painted in shades which could never be called subtle. Instead of an eagle propping up the pages on the lectern there's a pelican and Mortlock reckons that the four little lions at the corners of the c12 font look decidedly 'morning after the night before'.

TF 95402 12203
Dereham Road, Scarning, Dereham NR19 2PE

## SCOTTOW All Saints

This is a church full of curious things, most curious of all being the font cover. Many font covers are dainty and delicate – this one is robust. Green fishes the height of the cover, with smiles on their faces, serve as handles. The whole looks heavy and since there's a step and a half up to the font it must be quite a tricky job taking the cover off without dropping it. Other curiosities include a splendid Green Man on a boss in the porch, an oak double sided swivelling lectern and the Royal Arms of our present Queen – a rarity, one wonders if the near proximity of the former RAF Coltishall had anything to do with that.

TG 26530 23761
Church Road, Scottow, Norwich NR10 5DF

## SCULTHORPE All Saints

In 1381 the new Lord of the Manor began rebuilding the ruined church. Is this why the tower is in a less than usual place (on the south side but not at the western end) – maybe the tower was in good enough shape to be reused but it suited the restorers to place it unconventionally. This is not the only example of a strangely placed tower, at Edgefield (*Norfolk Churches from the Air*) for instance, the tower was built almost twenty five years after the rebuilt church and tacked on to the NE corner where it looks odd. There has been a great deal of Victorian restoration here but most noteworthy perhaps are the stained glass windows from the workshops of William Morris and Burne Jones. The font is a Norman gem depicting the Adoration of the Magi.

TF 89946 31871
Creake Road, Sculthorpe, Fakenham NR21 9NJ

# SHIMPLING St George

This small church is now the care of the Churches' Conservation Trust. The Norman tower is now restrained with two iron bands, the octagonal top was added c15 and the Victorian lead spire in 1863. The c16 timber- framed north porch is infilled with brick. It's a pretty church with lovely proportions and would be even more so had not the nave and chancel outside walls been covered by cement render.

TL 85962 51288
Aveley Lane, Shimpling, Diss IP21 4HF

## **SHOTESHAM** St Mary (at Hawes Green)

Until 1731 Shotesham had four churches in four parishes. Two remain, All Saints and St Mary's. St Mary's is away from the main village and is just a field away from the ruined St Martin's, St Botolph's is now just a heap of stones). St Mary's was renovated in 1879 (new roof, new floor, new pews). At the east end of the nave there's a Sanctus bell turret, the bell was rung to tell workers in the fields that it was time to stop and pray until its function ceased to be relevant.

TM 23778 98811
Hawes Green, Shotesham, Norwich NR15 1UW

## SIDESTRAND St Michael and All Angels

In 1841 the original tower fell down. A shorter tower replaced it temporarily and it was decided to move the whole building inland. This was carried out in 1881 except for the replacement tower and the rood staircase. The church was moved stone by stone and included some headstones from the old churchyard. Quite an achievement. And to prove the wisdom of Sir Samuel Hoare's decision the temporary tower, having been left on the cliff top, fell onto the beach in 1916. What a pity that rebuilding didn't happen at Eccles too. The original churchyard gained fame as Clement Scott's 'Garden of Sleep' in his writings in the 1880's.

TG 25951 39712
Cromer Road, Sidestrand, Cromer NR27 0NJ

## SOUTH BURLINGHAM St Edmund

South and North Burlingham, each with their own church, are two separate parishes about a mile and a half apart, separated by the busy A47 and the village of Lingwood, and they belong in separate benefices. Of St Edmund's Pevsner says the pulpit,'an exceptionally pretty Perpendicular piece' whilst Mortlock and Roberts declare it 'the finest c15 example in Norfolk' so all in all the pulpit is worth a visit but there are so many other treasures in this church. Adrian Pye (see Bibliography) writes 'It is as if the Victorians forgot this church existed…' (Halleluia!) The benches in the nave have carvings of animals in action (a fox with a goose over its shoulder, an elephant with a castle on its back). In the chancel there's a large painting of the martyrdom of Thomas à Becket (discovered 1856) and a faint St Christopher opposite the south door. Best to visit on a Churches Open Day.

TG 37242 08240
Church Road, South Burlingham, Norwich NR13 4EU

## SOUTH WALSHAM St Mary and St Lawrence

Two churches in one churchyard is not as rare as one might think and at Reepham (*Norfolk Churches form the Air*) there are three churches although one of those is in ruins.

St Mary, of c15, has a magnificent tower. In the sanctuary near the altar there's a stone slab from the tomb of a c15 Abbot of St Benet's having been used in the meantime as a doorstep in the palace of the Duke of Norfolk in Norwich. The palace has long disappeared. St Mary's is fully functioning.

St Lawrence over the years has been unfortunate. Built c15, in 1827 the thatched building caught fire and was gutted. Rebuilding resulted in a chancel and a nave smaller than the original. The destruction continued in the 1970's when there was a partial collapse of the tower after which a sonic boom finished the job unintentionally leaving St Lawrence's considerably reduced in area but still functioning and keeping the status of a church. Today it has become an arts venue with modern facilities together with a herb garden and has never been deconsecrated.

TG 36527 13223
The Street, South Walsham, Norwich NR13 6DQ

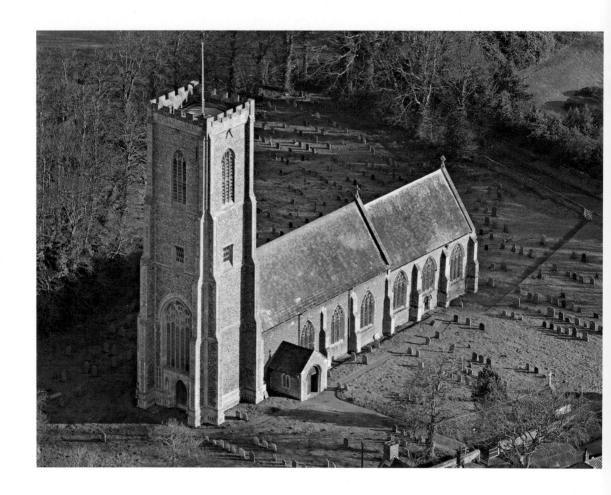

## SOUTHREPPS St James

This large church was even larger before the aisles were demolished in 1791. The 114 foot high tower built 1448 has scallop shells (the emblem of St James) around its base  and its sound holes have unusually delicate tracery. Inside there's some modernisation but although the Victorians renovated the top of the rood screen, the base panels are original  and remain as diaper squares of red  and green.

TG 25665 36764
Clipped Hedge Lane, Southrepps, Norwich NR11 8NZ

# SOUTHWOOD St Edmund

Sadly ruined churches are a common occurrence in Norfolk. This modest one ceased to be used in the 1880s and the congregation worshipped at Limpenhoe instead.

TG 39140 05326
Norwich Road, Southwood, Norwich NR13 3LS,

## STALHAM St Mary

The church is at the end of the High Street so very much part of the town. The tower is squat much like the tower at Stratton Strawless. Inside, the eye goes straight to the c15 octagonal stone font which is massive and stands on a plinth of three steps. Worth seeking out is part of the rood screen now on the chancel's south wall. It contains a picture of a hardly known saint, St Roche. French, he died in 1355 and on his image he's showing the plague scars on his left leg. He had a reputation for reducing the effects of the plague wherever he went but he attracted the attention of the wrong people and ended up in prison where he died accused of being a spy.

TG 37300 25135
High Street, Stalham, Norwich NR12 9AQ

## STOKE HOLY CROSS The Holy Cross

Architect Thomas Jeckyll in 1872 carried out a whole makeover of the c13 church so there's precious little left from earlier dates except a couple of carved bench ends with a bear and what might be a monkey. The WWI memorial could have come straight from the workshops of William Morris, it's a triptych with St Michael and St George surrounding a list of the fallen – a lovely piece. And outside there's a memorial to Thomas Havers, died 1917, clergyman, doctor, surgeon and 'cutting for the stone' (did this mean he was also a sculptor, a stone mason or did he specialise in the removal of gall stones?) Beneath his 'details' are relief sculptures of the tools of his trade – they're a bit sparse – a modern handyman would have a more comprehensive collection but they add interest to the churchyard. A mystery remains – in the churchyard in a corner next to the tower there's an ancient font (planted with bulbs) Maybe inside the church there's an explanation but the church was locked.

TG 23540 00790
Norwich Road, Stoke Holy Cross NR14 8AB

## STOKESBY St Andrew

The parish is also known as Stokesby-cum-Herringsby. The oldest part is the flint tower but the rest of this visually appealing church is of red brick, except for the stone work surrounding the run of nine windows of the clerestory (clear storey). Shelton Hall and the church were built simultaneously by Sir Ralph Shelton but unlucky family links caused further development to stop. His son had married the aunt of Henry VIII's second wife Anne Boleyn and when that unfortunate queen was beheaded her daughter, the future Elizabeth I, fled to Shelton Hall. She sought refuge in the church tower when her life was in danger.

TG 43542 10649
Filby Road, Stokesby, Great Yarmouth NR29 3ET

## STOW BEDON St Botolph

The bell cote has been described as having a 'candle snuffer top' and that's exactly what it looks like. It's difficult to date this church. Pevsner lists Norman, Perpendicular and Decorated windows and in 1740 it had a square tower but this had disappeared by 1820. When c19 remedial work was done there were indications that the church was built c13 or earlier. On the four inch thick stone mensa table there are five Consecration crosses, the crosses marked the places where the Bishop had sprinkled oil at the ceremony of the church's consecration. In 1967 the church was restored to its present state.

TL 96190 95602
Gravelpit Hill, Stow Bedon, Attleborough NR17 1BX,

## STRATTON ST MICHAEL St Michael

The tower is squat, without buttresses and doesn't reach up to a belfry stage – there's a a bell turret topped off with a spirelet instead. The nave and chancel (c14) are one but there's a change in the roof elevation where the screen begins. The rood stair with a door is in the north wall. The rarest feature in this church would have been the beautifully crafted altar rail which would have enclosed the altar on three sides (a c17 device – there are only three others in Norfolk at Thurning, Merton and West Dereham) but at some stage it's been sawn leaving only the front rail in place (the cut off portions went for 'indifferent' choir stall fronts). Pity.

TM 20476 93658
Church Lane, Long Stratton, Norwich NR15 2QB

## STRATTON STRAWLESS St Margaret

'Stratton' means a settlement (*tun*) on a Roman road. Strawless? No idea but in a grain growing county like Norfolk to be without straw seems unlikely.

The c15 tower is exceedingly 'chunky' and the idea has been mooted that perhaps it was intended to go higher but the plan must have changed because there are seated figures at each corner of the battlements. Here are monuments both inside and out to the Marsham family of Stratton Strawless Hall, a screen across the south aisle changed it into a chapel for those monuments. Among them there's a sad chrysom baby, Margaret Marsham in her swaddling clothes. There are earlier monuments too, some goulish. Most striking of the church treasures is a magnificent c18 chandelier with twenty five branches and thought to be Russian. It was given to the church by W J Birkbeck (d1916) a successive owner of the Hall who was a great friend of the Russian Orthodox church.

A mystery yet to be solved is the fact that the village of Marsham is only a couple of miles down the road but neither the village nor the c14 church seems to have any connection with the Marsham family. Strange.

TG 22192 20772

Church Road, Stratton Strawless, Norwich NR10 5LN

# SUTTON St Michael

The c14 tower has stains from the iron ties holding in the tower, which is a pity. Otherwise the church is spick and span and well cared for if somewhat plain and clearly a recipient of the Victorian 'makeover' which, to be fair, has ensured that the church's life is extended. Possibly those Victorian 'improvers' couldn't win. The east window with its restrained geometric design and Biblical figures above is Victoriana to a tee. One of the best bits is the Tudor porch, especially the entrance which clearly once had an upper floor (a parvise).

TG 38885 23950
Church Road, Sutton, Norwich NR12 9SA

## SWAINSTHORPE St Peter

The angels in the roof are rather splendid and appear to be in very good condition, it's possible their wings have at some time been replaced but the bodies are original. The problem of how to fit a whole angel in corner space only big enough for half an angel is solved neatly by slicing each in half from head to toe ... gives a whole new meaning to wings being clipped.
The tower is probably Saxon with a c14 octagonal top added.

TG 21920 00968
Church Road, Swainsthorpe NR14 8PH

## SWANTON MORLEY All Saints

This is a magnificent c14/15 church with massive Perpendicular windows on the south side, octagonal piers of the tower's base and its huge bell openings. Parson James Woodforde (1740-1803) famous for his '*Diary of a Country Parson*' used to ride over to Swanton Morley from Weston Longville to buy his writing paper, one wonders how often he came into this church. Much of the window glass in clear which makes this a light, bright church but there's a coloured window dedicated to RAF Swanton Morley which was a huge grass airfield active 1940-1995. There's a section in the churchyard dedicated to RAF personnel stationed here who lost their lives during this period.

TG 01897 17307
Mill Street, Swanton Morley, Dereham NR20 4PB

## SWANTON NOVERS St Edmund

There are three Swantons in Norfolk – Abbot, Morley and Novers. Swanton was the *tun* or dwelling of swineherds, Novers was held by Milo de Nuiers (and his swineherds) in 1200. The tower was rebuilt in 1821 and again in 1960. According to Mortlock and Roberts the villagers reckoned that 'one good hard kick' would demolish it. Fortunately no one did (kick the tower) and although demolition would have been the easier option the parishioners set about restoring the entire church using the original materials whenever possible. They were dealing with a church probably of Norman origin. Fonts, being generally of stone and moveable, have often survived in churches when most of the other furnishings have gone and so it is here. It has c15 stone carvings bearing the ox of Luke, the man of Matthew, the lion of Mark and the eagle of John, all winged.

TG 01553 32383
Church Lane, Swanton Novers, Melton Constable NR24 2RF

# TAVERHAM St Edmund

An octagonal top was added to the Norman tower in the 15th century. The nave and chancel roof were both thatched but a fire in 1970 resulted in a tile substitute on the nave. Round the fine c14 font are figures of saints. Fragments of a c14 screen, possibly from another church, now form an altar rail with a modern 'out of keeping' rail at the top.

TG 16041 13848
Costessey Road, Taverham, Norwich NR8 6SY

# THARSTON St Mary

The stair turret to the belfry is easy to spot on the outside of the tower as is the Consecration Cross on the south wall near the door. Consecration Crosses marked the areas where the Bishop splashed anointed oil on the fabric of the new church inside and out to bless it. Both the church and churchyard are full of the Harvey family of Tharston Hall. Outside there's a mausoleum (foreground of picture) inside there are several marble monuments to the Harveys, the most striking being that of General Sir Robert Harvey who fought in the Napoleonic Wars. On either side of his tribute there are two soldiers dressed in the uniforms of the day. There's also a spooky monument to c17 Robert Wood portrayed as a recumbent skeleton. The Honours List of WWI and WWII is worked in marble. And three of the bench ends at the front of the nave are beautifully carved – one is a king with a crown but carries a bishop's crozier, next to him there's a crowned and winged lady with attendant angels and opposite there's an angel holding the scales of judgement – in one scale pan there's a devil and in the other a repentant sinner.

TM 19013 94325
Hall Lane, Tharston, Norwich NR15 2YG

# THELVETON St Andrew

The church was originally Norman but most of the existing fabric is c14 and was heavily restored by the Victorian Mann family. The tower fell in 1757, note the bell turret and single bell. The Mann family restoration includes the introduction of a marble reredos behind the altar, carpeting and chairs throughout. The c15 font remains untouched. On the chancel wall there's a portrait of Thomas Mann and the inscription:

'Born at The House, Albion Brewery, Mile End Road Road … owner of the Thelveton Estate which parish he entirely remodelled. He zealously promoted Religious and Secular education also the moral and social welfare of his tenants and labourers.'

TM 15164 81326
Church Road, Thelveton, Diss IP21 4EP

# THOMPSON St Martin

In the year of the Black Death (1349) a college of canons was founded here and their order continued until the Dissolution. It's possible that their founding was concurrent with the building of the church. Of the interior Mortlock and Roberts say 'A calm and lovely interior with oak pews the colour of old cider'. This is essentially a 'homely' church, the flowers on the rood screen could have been the inspiration for a wallpaper design by Laura Ashley. The pulpit and the clerk's desk look somewhat home made and cobbled together from bits of timber found around the church. And none the worse for that.

TL 92989 96923
Church Lane, Thompson, Thetford IP24 1QE

## THORPE-NEXT-HADDISCOE St Matthias

This is a little gem tucked away on the marshes between the Rivers Yare and Waveney. From the tower's base to the top of the strange pillars it's Saxon, the Norman windows of the top third of the tower are bricked up (without explanation) to half their height. The porch came later but the south door into the church is Norman also. The red brick chancel of 1836 is a replacement. The font is Norman, large, square and without decoration except for arcading which explains why it wasn't defaced by the iconoclasts, Cromwell's men.

TM 43577 98105
North End, Thorpe-next-Haddiscoe, Norwich NR14 6PY

## THRIGBY St Mary

On the c14 tower the two visible bell openings are of the same period but of different design and the two round the back are different again. Very odd. No explanation. The church was extensively restored in the 1890s but features left intact are the c14 doorway with floral motifs on the moulded arch, the Royal Arms of King George III, two Consecration Crosses and a square recess oven (with flue) at the base of the tower where communion wafers were baked.

TG 46033 12402
Thrigby Road, Filby, Great Yarmouth NR29 3DS

## THURLTON All Saints

This is a handsome thatched church with decorative flintwork at the top, in the base course of the tower and on the porch. On the south side there's a Norman doorway with typical zig zag moulding and also a rood stair turret. Victorian architect Thomas Jeckyll carried out a restoration here in the 1850s as he did in so many other Norfolk churches. Here he reglazed the windows, reclad the roofs, inserted a new window into the tower and refloored the attractive porch. Inside he repaired the font and added a new base and stair to the pulpit. Next to the pulpit there's a traditional hour glass stand, the hour glass was like a giant egg timer, after the Reformation sermons were particularly long. Was the timer for the benefit of the priest or the congregation? The painted rood screen is particularly delicate, the panels have been removed, probably by iconoclasts after the Reformation. The St Christopher on the north wall is well preserved.

TM 41713 98332
Church Road, Thurlton, Norwich NR14 6RL

## THURNE All Saints

The c14 tower has a squint (a peep hole) at eyelevel in the west wall of the tower. From the inside it's possible to see the ruins of St Benet's Abbey across the marshes. One theory is that the squint was there to summon help from the Abbey in times of need but would the light from one candle show up across a distance of a mile or so and what if help were needed during the day? And helpers would need to cross Thurne Dyke so was a boat kept handy in case of need? Looking through the squint from outside, the line of sight goes straight to the altar, maybe there was a sacramental point to all this. Otherwise there's no mystery here, the east window contains good examples of Victorian glass.

TG 40494 15604
Church Road, Thurne, Great Yarmouth NR29 3BT

# THURSFORD St Andrew

The church sits within the grounds of Thursford Hall (see also Merton). Apart from the c14 tower the rest was remodelled by the Chadd family of Thursford Hall  and is a bit of a Gothic extravaganza but the Victorian stained glass windows get Pevsner's approval. A most unusual siting is the Chadd family pew in the south transept six feet above floor level because the family mausoleum lies underneath.

TF 98384 33807
Heath Lane, Thursford, Fakenham NR21 0BW

## TITTLESHALL St Mary

Tower, nave and chancel are all c14. The large Coke mausoleum (off the chancel) is c18, used for a hundred and fifty years until a vault at Holkham was built in the 1870s. The church is full of Coke grand monuments but also there's an Honours Board listing the children who won scholarships from Tittleshall school. But as Simon Knott observes sadly several of the early names appear also on the WWI memorial. .

TF 89470 21083
Church Lane, Tittleshall, King's Lynn PE32 2PN,

# **TOFTREES** All Saints

Either the c15 tower was never completed or the top third has been demolished, its functional copper cap giving the tower an 'un-English' look. Inside is what is considered to be one of the finest Norman fonts in the county. Square, stone, solid with what Mortlock describes as 'barbaric animal heads at each corner and standing on five stumpy columns'. It could not be mistaken for a font of any other period. Outside there are the remains of a Churchyard or Preaching Cross where the resident priest or wandering friars would preach – there must have been a larger population in Toftrees in those days.

TF 89821 27576
Shereford Road, Toftrees, Fakenham NR21 7EA

## TROWSE aka **TROWSE NEWTON** St Andrew

This c13 church close to Norwich contains an extraordinary carving. Two angels and a king, all life size carved wooden figures with musical instruments (King David with his harp flanked by two angels blowing their trumpets) sit round the base of the pulpit – the gift of the Colman (mustard) family. It came from the base of a German organ. It must have been quite a relief to the family to find a home for such an extraordinary piece – and who can refuse a patron's wishes after all? The patronage itself is rather unusual because the Colman's were non-Conformists. In 1901 the family paid for a major restoration in the church following a flood. The River Yare flows close by the tower on its way to join the River Wensum less than a mile away. Other attributes are the east window tracery (but not the glass) a gift from Prior William of Norwich cathedral (1272-1288) and a c18 lectern with a pelican rather than the usual eagle.

TG 2448 0687
The Street, Trowse NR14 8SX

# TUNSTALL St Peter and St Paul

Mortlock describes the ruined tower 'its top like a rotten tooth'. By 1704 the church was in urgent need of repairs, no service had been held there for over forty years. In 1705 Mrs Elizabeth Jenkinson paid to have a wall built between the chancel and the ruined nave with the intention of enabling the chancel to be used again. Today one service a year is held in the chancel to ensure this church's continuity.

TG 41378 08506
Staithe Road, Tunstall, Norwich NR13 3PS

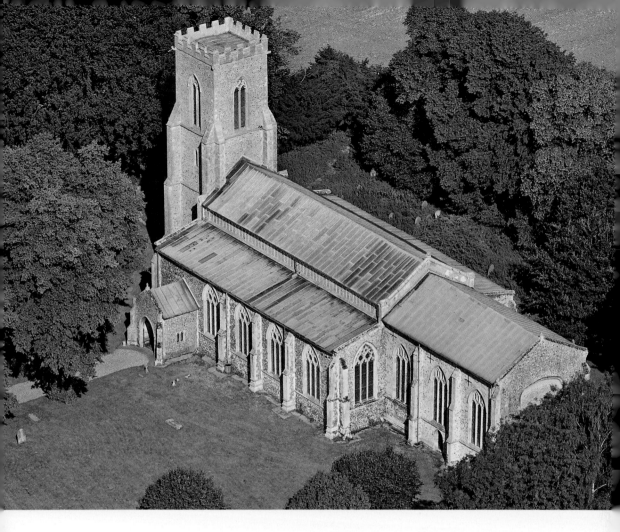

## TUNSTEAD St Mary

Building the church started in 1327 funded by the profits from the wool trade but the Black Death,1349, brought a stop to that and it wasn't until 1371 that work here began again. The rood screen is exceptional. Begun in 1470 and completed around 1490 it contains pictures of the four Latin Doctors and the Apostles and is the work of more than one artist. The rood floor and rood beam are intact although the rood (Christ on the Cross) is absent.

TG 30844 22677
Church Lane, Tunstead, Norwich NR12 8HU

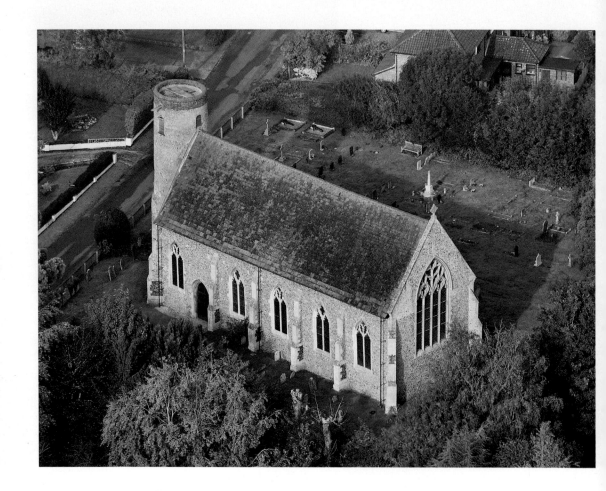

## WACTON All Saints

The tapering round tower dates from before the Conquest, the rest is c14. What remains of the screen is very plain and there are rood stairs leading to a rood loft.

TM 17968 91734
Bustards Green, Norwich NR15 2UG

# WALCOTT All Saints

Much of the Victorian restoration work here was masterminded by the Reverend Horatio Nelson William Comyn – godson of the famous Admiral and baptised on board HMS *Victory*. He was clearly an early entrepreneur who raised money for the restorations by selling tobacco, sweets etc from his pony and trap. An unusual feature of this c15 church is the V shaped stair turret. The c15 elaborate screen has been restored to great effect. An Art Nouveau lectern, sensibly, has been chained to the floor.

TG 36021 31734
Coast Road, Walcott, Norwich NR12 0PD

## WATLINGTON St Peter and St Paul

Many changes have taken place in this church since it was begun in the thirteenth century. The tower was given an extra storey (there's a change in the brickwork two thirds of the way up). A red brick staircase turret has been tacked on to the south side of the tower. 'Round the back' in all that is left now of a north chapel are two aumbries (small cupboards in which the holy oil was stored) and a piscina (a stone basin near the altar) both used in Holy Communion. These are now simply part of the main fabric. The roof line of the nave was changed and the outline of the former roof is clearly visible on the east wall of the tower. Inside there's evidence of craftsmanship both old and relatively new. And violence. The stone figures round the c16 font have all lost their heads. Victims of iconoclasm? The Jacobean font cover is tall but plain and lacking in the finesse and decoration of an earlier age. A talented c19 vicar restored the screen and added to the figures on the bench ends. All in all a rather interesting church.

TF 62108 11171
Church Road, Watlington, King's Lynn PE33 0HE

# WEASENHAM ST PETER St Peter

There are two Weasenham parishes, St Peter and All Saints. Both churches are of c 13/14 origin. St Peter is described as being in Lower Weasenham, a contradiction ecclesiastically because St Peter is considered to be a high church figure. Most striking is the carved and coloured reredos of the south chapel. Battlements along the roof of the main church and south chapel (and tower) add to the solidity of the whole although it seems strange that there are no clerestory windows to admit light into the nave. In the churchyard is the grave and headstone of broadcaster John Timpson who died in 2005.

TF 85607 22367
Fakenham Road, Weasenham St Peter, King's Lynn PE32 2TF

## WEST DEREHAM St Andrew

This church has the largest diameter round tower of any in Norfolk (17 feet internally at ground level with walls four feet thick), the octagonal top was built c16. Originally there were two churches here, the rubble of the other one has disappeared amid the gravestones and there was also an Abbey of the White Friars founded in 1188 but dissolved in that tumultuous year 1536. The main fabric of the church is possibly even older than the tower although the main windows are later, from the Perpendicular period (c14-15). The chancel was restored 1895 and soon afterwards the nave roof collapsed and had to be restored also (seemingly not everything the Victorians did to churches was of their own volition!) In this church is what Mortlock describes as 'one of the best standing monuments in Norfolk'. It's a life size marble of Colonel the Hon Edmund Soane (1706) wearing armour and a shoulder-length wig. His inscription says he was 'immaturely cut of (off) when he was in pursuit of and ready to be raised to the highest military honours'

TF 66730 02080
St Andrews Walk, West Dereham, King's Lynn PE33 9RT

## WEST HARLING All Saints

The Churches Conservation Trust took over this lovely building in 1976. The chancel is late c13 and there are corner stones (quoins) showing a former chapel to the south, demolished in 1733. The c14 tower had a stone spire until 1756. Unusually the rood stairs remain, perhaps that is precisely why the Trust took over this church and the fact that here there's the rarity of altar rails on three sides (only two other Norfolk churches have them – Thurning and Merton). The floor reveals a ledger stone to three successive rectors of the Cressener family, they served the parish for a continuous one hundred and thirty years.

TL 97397 85161
Unnamed Road, West Harling, Norwich NR16 2SE

## WEST RAYNHAM St Margaret

This church was in use for only three hundred years from c14. The Raynham estate restored East Raynham church (next to the entrance to Raynham Hall) in 1868 so presumably the then ruin of West Raynham church was allowed to decay still further. But fairly recently the decay has been slowed down, the tops of the walls are sealed so that damp no longer pervades and the ivy which covered it extensively has been cut away. A font (possibly the original) and a brick built altar have been installed so open air services can be held here.

TF 87952 25482
The Street, West Raynham, Fakenham NR21 7ER

## WEST SOMERTON St Mary

There are c11 walls incorporated into the c14 nave so the original church is of Norman origin including the tower which has a c14 top. The chancel is rather sparse compared to the thatched nave and it came later, possibly as much as five hundred years later. Every aspect of the chancel seems different in character to the nave (different roof and window treatment, larger windows, a shorter roof depth, different shaped buttresses). There are traces of medieval wall paintings in the nave, the clearest of which is the Last Judgement. The churchyard is best known for containing the tomb of Robert Hales, the Norfolk Giant but also in the churchyard is an epitaph to a good lady who 'toiled and muddled through her life'. I think we can all relate to that.

TG 47486 19570
Church Lane, West Somerton, Great Yarmouth NR29 4DR,

## WICKMERE St Andrew

The feature which catches the eye after taking in the round tower is the clerestory windows - their alternating design makes them both unusual and attractive. Did the stonemason or flint craftsman persuade the clergy or was this some whim of a c15 patron? The south porch also is faced with flint, the ironwork on the door is c14. The lumps of carstone at the tower's base and in the west wall indicates Saxon origin. When Wolterton church became a ruin three centuries ago the Walpoles (whose best known member was England's first Prime Minister Sir Robert Walpole) adopted Wickmere church. Both outside and in it contains tombs and memorials and the family hatchments (coats of arms).

TG 16544 33728
Watery Lane, Wickmere, Norwich NR11 7NB

# WIGGENHALL ST GERMANS St Germaine

Fenland churches seem to have a special quality. The big churches like Terrington St Clement and Walpole St Peter (see *Norfolk Churches from the Air*) have a cathedral-like splendour but even some of the more modest churches (as here) contain excellent craftsmanship. At St German's the medieval bench ends with their intricate carvings are fine examples of the wood carver's art with animals aplenty and some saints too. St Germans aka St Germanus aka St Germaine was a French c5 Bishop who among other 'miracles' enabled (allegedly on English soil) the English army to scare away the attacking Picts and Saxons merely by raising arms and yelling 'Alleluia' at them (wimps). Next to the raised banks of the River Ouse and lower than the water level, St Germans and the entire village is at risk from flooding. Climate change wasn't a factor when the Fens were drained but thanks to the St German's Pumping Station the church ( and village) should be safe from flooding today.

TF 59690 14018
Lynn Road, Wiggenhall St Germans, King's Lynn PE34 3EU

## **WINFARTHING** St Mary

The attractive place name conjures up old gentlemen playing ancient games on the village green. The Oxford Dictionary of English Place Names gives a literal translation as 'Wina's quarter'. Presumably Wina was a Viking who sensibly settled down here. The origin of many East Anglian place names came from the Viking marauders who raped, pillaged, liked what they saw  and stayed. A farthing was one quarter of a pre-decimal penny; in this instance it is probably from being a fourth part of an estate. Mystifying is the legend of 'The Good Swerde (sword) of Winfarthing' which stood for years in the chapel of the south aisle. It's assumed a thief dropped it there  and it acquired a mystic status … until it disappeared.

TM 10912 85723
Church Lane, Winfarthing, Diss IP22 2EA

# WITTON St Margaret

This is the St Margaret's Witton near North Walsham not to be confused with the St Margaret's Witton five miles east of Norwich. Two small round windows in the north wall indicate that at least part of the church was of Saxon origin as were the lower reaches of the tower. The building material of the tower changes as it ascends then red brick is included among the flint. It appears that the entrance to the tower has been inserted into the fabric of the west wall of the nave, the door leads to a staircase. One of the wall brasses commemorates Thomas Parmenter who died 12 days before Hollymus 1631. Hollymas aka Christmas – holly meaning holy rather than the prickly green stuff.

TG 33049 31592
Bacton Road, North Walsham NR28 9TS

## WOLTERTON St Margaret

The tower is all that remains of the church in the grounds of Wolterton Hall on the Mannington estate. Built in its entirety in the late c13 (i.e. the top was not added later as was often the case) the church was abandoned c18 to provide an open view from Wolterton Hall  and headstones were removed from the churchyard to enhance the landscaping.

TG 16347 32056
East Lodge, Wolterton Hall, Wolterton, Norwich NR11 7LY

## WORTHING St Margaret

This is a sad little church along a lane leading to nowhere. The Norman tower was capped with a red brick parapet when it was lowered to the height of the nave. The chancel had gone by 1820. The south door arch is a splendid example of Norman architecture but the modern door is locked and the nave windows are glazed with frosted glass so it's impossible to see in.

TF 99527 19528
Church Road, Worthing, Dereham NR20 5HR

## YAXHAM St Peter

This is a lovely little church. The tower is the oldest part and older than many other round towers, the clue is in the lumps of carstone (gingerbread stone) near the base deeming it to be of Saxon rather than Norman origin. On the west inside wall there's a door into the tower about twenty feet above the ground bearing out the theory that round towers were defensive devices. Most of the remainder of the church was built c14 or c15 although the clerestory windows belong to c19. Some of the bench ends have attractive animal carvings. The screen is modern and there's a modern rood suspended from the ceiling rather than sitting on a rood beam (platform) as was customary originally. In the 19th century the design of the c14 font was copied for Cromer church.

TG 00734 10681
Church Road, Yaxham, Dereham NR19 1RF

# Bibliography

Chatfield, Mark *Churches the Victorians Forgot* Moorland 1979
Collins *Guide to English Parish Churches* 1958
Dymond, David *The Norfolk Landscape* Alastair Press 1990
Groves, Nicholas *The Medieval Churches of the City of Norwich* HEART 2010
Harrod, Wilhemine *The Norfolk Guide* Alastair Press 1988
Hurst, Paul and Haselock, Jeremy *Norfolk Rood Screens* Philimore 2012
Jenkins, Simon *England's Thousand Best Churches* Allen Lane 1999
Malster, Robert *Maritime Norfolk Parts One* and *Two* Poppyland 2012 and 2013
Meeres, Frank *Not of this World* Blackall 2001
Messent, Claude, J W *Lych-gates and their churches in Eastern England* 1970
Mortlock, D.P. and Roberts, C.V. *Guide to Norfolk Churches* Lutterworth Press 2007
Pevsner, Nikolaus *The Buildings of England North West and South Norfolk* Penguin 1977
Pevsner, Nikolaus *The Buildings of England North East Norfolk and Norwich* Penguin 1977
Pye, Adrian *The Parish Churches of East Norfolk* ASPYE 2010
Pye, Adrian *The Parish Churches of Central Norfolk* ASPYE 2010
Pye, Adrian *The Parish Churches of West Norfolk* ASPYE 2010
Shreeve and Stilgoe *The Round Tower Churches of Norfolk* Canterbury Press 2001
Storey, Neil *The Lost Coast of Norfolk* The History Press 2009
Strong, Roy *A Little History of the English Country Church* Vintage 2007
Taylor, Richard *How to Read a Church* Rider 2003
Tilbrook and Roberts *Norfolk's Churches Great and Small* Jarrold 1997

# Index